The Conscience Market

by

James Christopher Pitts

authorHOUSE™

1663 LIBERTY DRIVE, SUITE 200
BLOOMINGTON, INDIANA 47403
(800) 839-8640
WWW.AUTHORHOUSE.COM

First published by AuthorHouse 03/05/05

ISBN: 1-4208-3271-9 (sc)

Library of Congress Control Number: 2005901372

Printed in the United States of America
Bloomington, Indiana

This book is printed on acid-free paper.

Table of Malcontent

Acknowledgements

To my wife, Lisa, for putting up with my endless ranting, and showing unfaltering love and support for me and my artistic vision, even when it conflicted so strongly with her own best judgment and beliefs. I apologize for the moments that I fail you. I appreciate the great job you did on the cover photos, too.

To my daughter, Savannah, for representing the purity of the next generation with poise and beauty exceeding her young age: you give me hope and light in the darkest of times.

To the Reverend Christopher Hein, Angela and Katrina, for loyalty beyond everyday friendship. Extra thanks are in order to Christopher for fully realizing the cover concept that was in my head. You are such an honest and gifted artist.

To Jim and Barbara Broyles, for intellectual guidance and input, and incredible conversations on any tangible subject, as well as many intangible theories.

To the most hilarious man I have ever had the pleasure of working with, Michael Prescott. Thanks for listening to my gripes and bitches, while simultaneously keeping me sane and somewhat grounded. Michael is one of the few to have previewed The Conscience Market, and his stand-in editorial contribution was essential more than once.

To my entire family, not because any of them have necessarily contributed to this project, but because their love and understanding have helped me to see more than one side to every issue.

To my best friends that have not already been mentioned: Jerry Twyford, Aaron Roten, Alex Arellano, and Chris Small. As well as the plethora of musicians that I have had the opportunity to record and perform with; there are too many to name here.

To my unconditionally adoring dog, Amos, you are a big sweetie!

To the Bush Administration, for such an endless amount of verbal ammunition. I hope in advance that the financially absurd inaugural back-patting was a grand success. Rest assured though, despite the unrelenting attack of your policies, I remain independent and in control of my decisions.

To The Reader:

As I prepare to send the final manuscript of the book you now hold in your hand, and what a time-bending concept that seems to expose, there are many events of incredible importance happening in this world of ours. I would like to take a moment to comment on some of the most pertinent to the near future of cause and effect; this is an opportunity to frame this anthology within the boundaries of its own time.

It is barely over a week since a magnitude nine earthquake beneath the Indian Ocean unleashed a devastating tsunami upon Indonesia, Thailand, Sri Lanka, and India, finding its way even to the tip of Somalia. The death toll at the time of this writing has reached over one hundred fifty thousand, and with disease, famine, and the on-going body count, that number could easily double. The most amazing thing happens at moments of utmost tragedy: people come together to help one another. Whatever ulterior motivations might be involved internationally and politically, the benefit is nevertheless felt. Everyday men and women (and some elephants) evolve momentarily and heroism is more than a vain war-time concept. This disaster has been no exception, with perhaps one of the most massive and far-reaching relief efforts the world has ever seen. Despite bickering sensitivities over who is or is not being "stingy", I for one am proud of the efforts made thus far to relieve the misery of what is truly an international tragedy, a horror felt even upon shores that were left untouched. The sad thing is that goodwill needs tragic events to provoke its influence.

There are also two impending elections of consequence: the scheduled, but possibly ill-fated, January 30th elections in Iraq and the January 9th election of a new Palestinian leader to replace the recently deceased Yassir Arafat. The repercussions of these two historic events could be of astonishing significance to the future, as well as any fading hope for Middle Eastern peace to come. As for Iraq, the insurrection has exploded (bad pun, however originally unintentional, and risking redundancy) in the last few weeks, with "improvised exploding devices"—or, as most people would call them, bombs—of the vehicular, road side, and vest-borne variety seeming to create havoc on a daily basis. One would have to be much more optimistic than I am to see the current state of affairs in Iraq as anything even approaching an accomplished mission, or a successful democracy building experiment. At least the war was quick, right? The only thing for me to say in relation to the Palestinian situation is that I hope a reasonable man is given the control, and ultimately the fate, of their plight. Extremity and terrorism will only beget more of the same, and

Israel is a powerful enemy, insured by the might of American weaponry and influence. There are only two choices: peace or more of the same.

Now, having placed you, the reader, directly into the current events as I type this, I will properly introduce the premise of the book. Much of what is to follow was written within the years of 2002-2004, and is primarily politically and philosophically assertive and controversial. Unfortunately, it is impossible to keep up to date with political discourse in writing, although I rest assured that political corruption is an eternal phenomenon and all rebellion against it remains relevant, whatever the time of its release.

With this being an anthology, there are also works dating all the way back to a bitter heartbroken young man in the '90's; what a poor unfortunate hack I was then. However, growth is essential and I find no shame in showing the evidence of mine. I have also included song lyrics from my tenure in the extreme progressive metal band, Scholomance, including some previously unpublished ones.

The material contained herein represents many aspects of everyday life in which I find it necessary to lend my own brand of social commentary. While the process and emotion involved in such creative endeavors is very personal in nature, the extremity of certain of these works is an exercise in symbolism, and at the same time an honest representation of repressed social and subconscious tendencies.

Therefore, I do not wish for you to make rash assumptions, overly literal interpretations, or archaic inquisitional judgments of the occasionally violent nature of my writing. Waste no time pondering the psychological implications that I was, or was not, attempting to convey.

This is art. Art has a responsibility to be honest and creative simultaneously. Appreciate the following for what it is—nothing more, nothing less. Works about love, betrayal, humor, spite, anger, war, religion, and a genuine desire for cultural renaissance await you the reader...

"Have nothing to do with the fruitless deeds of darkness, but rather expose them" – Ephesians 5:11

James C. Pitts – January 5th, 2005

By the way, Mahmoud Abbas was elected by the Palestinians on January 9th, with the promise of rehabilitated peace talks with Israel and the push for dual state recognition. The election was astonishingly without mass aggression and chaos, if the news is at all accurate.

The Abu Ghraib prison abuse trials are set to begin. Meanwhile, the man behind the memos, the honorable Judge Alberto Gonzales, will soon be our new Attorney General. This provides a supreme example of duplicity in action.

Also, there are threats coming in from Banda Aceh, Indonesia of renewed violence due to their ongoing separatist rebellion; if true, this could prove a shameful threat to relief workers and foreigners attempting to provide aid to Tsunami victims. What a gratuitous escalation of potential calamity this could all prove to be. The danger of child exploitation looms darkly over the region as well, with anxiety that some would use this time of misfortune to enslave and prostitute the helpless orphaned victims. I suppose this type of lunacy provides a fitting milieu to the social-political rant you are about to encounter upon turning the page…

Updated on January 9th, 2005

<u>Section One</u>

Against Fundamentalism, Intolerance, and Excessive Hubris

The Conscience Market

Teach your children to fear me, but you are the ones who would murder their spirit. Cast the crooked finger of aspersion upon me while resting under the protection of a criminal heroism. So consumed with arrogance that an atrocious lie is preferential to an undeniable truth; whatever it takes to emit the perception of Honor. ...An exchange of Soul Eternal, of Human Spirit, for financial status. Glorify the tithe; trade your very nature for a deceptive order. To follow an order? ...Chaos the bastard of that deadbeat father.

Societal marionette—
Dance the dance, mime the emotion;
Ruled by strings and ever floating.
"What would the Master have me do?"

Always as he commands: worship the idol of banners, carry out the necessary ritual of a birth given only to be taken away. Go forth, multiply, condemn and die. The moral being: all systems emerge only to fail at the advent of human intervention.

2004

<u>Cruelty</u>

Never more than a word—not in any curse or hex or spell—or insinuation of death or sex or hell; thus the art of misdirection, born of fear and ignorance; not innocent of lust for power, of soul and spirit on which to devour—to utterly glut. Feast of fear—Feast of fear—Silence the science—Indict the seer!

No magic so black, nothing so vile, as this quest to quell any conscience, any fact, all insurrection.

Is it truly as it does? Was there ever growth in oppressive love? A resounding no! Away from revelation! Hands off you filth of judgment! I seek the meaning not the book.

Don't move to stone, or make me stoned—no light, no dark, no drugs, no lies. Drowning cult of idle idolatry—Make no threats, no claims on me—Outgrowth of tentacled cruelty—Suffocation of my humanity.

...Never more than a questionable word, an uncomfortable appearance, a thorn to lance enforced adherence.

Do you see? Hear? For the sake of the crucified, martyred, burned and drowned can you feel?

Who are you? Who am I? In two words: Cruelty Personified.

2004

James Christopher Pitts

A Lesson in Preemption

There's a fever spreading like wildfire, much to the approval of the good ol' fat cats. Ya know, the smiling loafs of vanity, men like Hannity, who lack humanity but condone insanity...

Ever the beneficiaries of a poor man's misfortune, the proprietors of gain compounded through others suffering; the aforementioned malady of Homeland Insecurity. Are they comin' after me (the innocent bed-ridden victim of greater faith in his country)?

The basis of preemption gone berserk, social classes in a war of status and out of work; it's just a fucking word!

What a concept these men have exploited: to attack in defense. And people believe it, they buy into it without the Patriotism to ask questions; always the same plea of 'defense'. Obviously not very attentive sports fans, this lot... What can you expect from a den of thieving lawyers?

We the people! We the people! Does not one soul remember?! Our rights further more dismembered. A recovery is due.

Take our future away from the Lobby. We cast the votes, will that ever matter again? Will the promise of the forefathers ever again be worth more than the paper it was written on?

My heart is breaking at the loss of illusory innocence, my repetitious theme, breaking over the exposure of so many poorly concealed conspiracies. Bring back our liberty. Give back our goddamned liberty!

Cease the partisan play before it reaches Shakespearean Tragedy. Resurrect her in the honor of boundless, though secular, unity.

Let him who pays taxes cast the first stone. And while we're waxing biblical and financial, I must say this: When God pays his fair share in taxes maybe his not-so-humble servants can justifiably influence politics. End of the Spin indeed.

This is my verbal act of preemption. My heightened paranoia has caused my words to stoop to that irrevocable level. Wait....that is simply not true.

They drew first when they infringed upon my freedom. That is a lesson in an indefensible act of insult—the theft of our choice. They drew first, I dare say. They always do.

2004

Of The Backstabbers, A Flimsy Moral Compass, & A Tedious Un-Patriotic Division

Where will you be when they come for the essence of all that you love, of your inner most thoughts? Will you relinquish your self too peacefully, turn tail and run, or stand to the death?

Does your assurance in friends, in God and Country, give way upon the slightest challenge, the least admonition? ...Another verification of a flawed concept of invisible conviction.

Right and Left conspiracy theorists fan the flames of the latest social inferno. No one seems to mourn the already scorched corpse of unity; a thorough desiccation I'm afraid. The Dregs of Divergence always resort to Playground name calling. Insecurity and immaturity revealed as they bicker like impotent adolescents: a Democratic free ride, a Republican war, another failed Independent—all betraying independence.

And we blame Art for our children's rebellious behavior. Where is the example of honesty better established than in artistic expression? This is but a political and religious platform, a grand diversion from the reality of the staggering incompetence of their authority, the concavity, the depravity, the base vanity of supposedly good influence.

There are really no good or bad influences. To influence is to remove one's opportunity to think objectively. But, that is the underlying intention after all; Dominion over choice and free will, Antagonism of creativity.

I sense a threat from within, a parasitic populace, a viral world government—Hell-bent on a homicidal quest for commerce, an eventual suicide for a moment of wealth; of power as the guest of subversion. Terror is accomplished with every right taken or given away; confirming the anxiety of those who would claim to preserve, as they amend to discriminate, the original deceptive promise of rich, white Slave masters proclaiming equality.

Where will you be when I come for your children; to tell them to never trade freedom for security; education for popularity? Will you measure up to your lectures of credence? Or will you continue to foster the bastard of untruth?

How will you feel as they storm through your country, assuming control, claiming your land and lives? Stripping the landscape of its resource and beauty, installing their puppet despot to rule...Of course, he too will be dealt with eventually; cyclical nature of Might at the beckon of the Heedless.

Where will I be when they come to my home; a final reckoning for the disenchanted exhorter? ...Resting well with a clear conscience.

2004

The Dread Voyeurs

I say good man, have you heard the latest news? Try not to breathe the air today, don't run outside there's acid rain—a chicken on every table, and all of them diseased.

What's the latest fright? Just tune on in, 10 at night!

Did you hear about the shootings, the bombs that daily drop? Did you see the black man run on 'Cops'?

The wars, the deaths, the genocide—but what about celebrity lives? Are Fuck and Fickle still together? Did Mr. Plastic marry Princess Fable?

The terror threat is elevated to orange or yellow or bullshit brown. Did you hear the plant is closing down? Not much to say on that, there's always more important flap.

We the media do solemnly swear to tell the partial truth, the sensationalized truth, the outright lies to viewers as dung to flies.

The political drivel is sprinkled in as blots of misleading impressionism. Impressions of the facts are all we need. Come ye Peons feed or bleed!

Are you scared today? Lock your doors and cock your pistol, but the enemy is still inside.

You watch them faithfully, every night.

2004

Patriotism

Does the banner wave on high? Has it been set about half mast; to mourn the loss of all our fallen, or just the loss of dreams? That is the mythical theme we strive to make ourselves believe. An apathetic view of honesty: unfair, unbalanced, biased opinions to weave insecurity.

A proud nation is a dangerous nation. Excessive hubris in tragedy agrees. Just ask the souls of Auschwitz, the Serbs, the Armenians, the Greeks. Interrogate the children of Kabul, Baghdad, or Tikrit. Or perhaps go ask the Navajo, or try to find a Cherokee.

Pride does not allow acceptance of responsibility. Stand together, yes, but not in denial. Future goals are dashed by blind knowledge of history.

Blue bloods, white men, red blood of red men, building our wealth on the backs of the blacks; freedom of religion, so long as it's Christian, allow the under-privileged to slip right through the cracks.

Exalted leaders of men to their graves, what is the honor of dying in vain? Forgotten tomorrow are all of the names of those who believed the rallying cries, to protect the interest of the wealthiest lives. Why do we follow a creed of self malevolence? ...To carry traditions of perpetual lies.

I do not hate my country. I hold its leaders to the standards in which they proclaim.

Practice patriotism with both eyes open.

2004

Compassionate Observations of Right and Wrong

I want to get George W. Bush something for Christmas, but, what do you get for the man who already takes everything?

Speaking of King George, I don't know whether to laugh or cry when he rattles off some poor excuse for a sentence about caring for the environment, or calls himself the education President. At least he was telling the truth for a change when he claimed to be a "war President". His dad must be so proud…

Guns don't kill people; People kill people…often with guns…And no I'm not a gun control nut you twitchy pistol fuckers!

Have you ever noticed how worried Christians are about the inevitable consequences of living; as in, for instance, the inexorableness of dying? Where is the confidence in God's divine plan, where is the confidence in the heavenly here-after?

Who told John Ashcroft that he could sing? The eagle may soar, however, his voice shouldn't attempt to.

Speaking of songs, have you heard that country anthem, "Independence Day" by Martina McBride, which Sean Hannity plays on his radio show? First things first: what are we declaring independence from Martina? I wish it was from foreign oil, or fear and terror, but if that were the case the song wouldn't be featured on the ultimate neo-conservative (and what an oxymoron that is—new and conservative!?) poster boy's radio show. The catchy little ditty begins with Martina belting out, "Let freedom ring!", which of course is an inspiring and worthy sentiment, it just seems to me that she should be singing "Let bullets ring", or "Let ears ring from the many bombs dropping during excessively propagandized and endless warfare", or something to that effect. I guess there's no pop 'cred' or nationalistic fanfare to be had with an honest representation of the song's intent. My favorite lines are the brilliantly contradictory pair about letting the white dove (presumably representative of Christ and/or peace) sing, eloquently rhymed with a line about it being a "day of reckoning". You know, I wanted revenge for 9/11 as much as the next guy, or gal in this case, yet I find it very difficult to stomach such overt contradictory garbage;

unless I write it of course…and then it's fucking brilliant! Oh, and don't get me started on the Ford shmuck man Toby Keith, or any of the other bastions of backwoods conveniently patriotic NASCAR fodder.

Who was the son of a bitch that decided you can't oppose a war without opposing the troops? These soldiers do not choose their deployment. Nor do they choose whether those in power utilize their services for only defensible positions. Do I think that we can just pull out and leave in the middle of the insurgency and re-building in Iraq? No, I actually don't. That doesn't change the lack of preparedness by our Defense Department. That doesn't excuse the arrogant rush into war made by the Bush Administration and the cowardice of Congress for accepting falsified intelligence indiscriminately in the aftermath of September 11th. I don't blame the troops for doing what they must in order to survive. I blame the ignorance that put them in such a compromising position in the first place. I truly feel for the troops and their families; in the future I would like to see the people who actually declare wars accept responsibility for their greed, deception, and ineptitude. I hope that Iraq is able to become a democratic nation and not just a convenient place for Generals to plant bases and stage battles from. If that element of the mission is accomplished, all credit should go to the men and women fighting and dying there, not to any posturing politicians playing hero.

Does it worry anybody else that Donald Rumsfeld has the audacity to let soldiers be court-martialed for plating their minimally armored vehicles with abandoned scrap equipment from other battalions in order to better survive while transporting supplies? Does it worry anyone that Rumsfeld, in his grandstanding incompetence, sent our soldiers to war without the proper equipment in the first place? How about the fact that he looks like a soulless demon-spawn zombie? …Anyone? There are also the issues of women in battle, the crafty drafting of discharged vets, and the use of un-insured soldiers from the National Guard (or was it the Reserves?) to be considered.

Back to Sean Hannity: When he says "Now more than ever, it's the Sean Hannity show", does that mean that he is more 'Sean Hannity' than he used to be? What was his level of 'Hannity Content' set at before?

I will definitely be despised by most anyone who reads my book. That is the consequence of being an opinionated prick. But, why aren't more people properly appreciating and displaying their freedoms of speech, religion, to assemble, of press? Those Rights are in force to keep America under the control of the ostensibly fabled "We". Of course, we have an often times obnoxious media, but their power is undeniable. To any members of the discriminatory press who may be reading this: Stop cheering on the Republicans and/or the Democrats with prior bias and do your damn job! If the press had spent half of the time on the fraudulent election of 2000, or the contrived evidence that led up to the war in Iraq, that they did on the ridiculous Clinton allegations, we wouldn't be in this mess. I guess sucking cock appeals to these cretins more than protecting people's rights and lives; more than safe-guarding our environmental conservation and our economy…In truth I believe we are all to blame for allowing that colossal waste of time and resources. Fuck you Ken Starr!

And while we're on the subject of sucking cock, if you don't want to be drafted tell the military that you're GAY. …Works every time.

This one goes directly to Karl Rove: Have you committed character assassination of any war heroes lately? Or, were you too busy propagating horrendous accusations about their adopted children? Mother Theresa would be so proud of your platform of pro-life mockery. In all fairness, I do wish that you were my publicist…Never mind, I'd rather retain the possession of my soul.

Just to be fair, what the hell was up with the handling of Waco's Branch Davidian sect under the Clinton Administration? That may be ancient history, but there is some frightening video floating around out there…

I think it's fucking hilarious that Rush Limbaugh is a pill freak. That's semi-old news; still he never ceases to amaze me with the boundlessness of his hypocrisy.

I heard Bill O'Reilly bitching about progressive thinking yesterday, meanwhile espousing his retrogressive traditionalist philosophy, and it made me downright flabbergasted. It is very difficult for me to accept the fact that progression is held in disdain by a majority of Americans. Sometime these bastards should look back at some of our more sadistic glorified traditions and reach the stunning conclusion that excessive tradition is stagnation and stagnation is death. Nothing matters without progress. Bill certainly wouldn't have the technology with which to spout his often asinine viewpoints without progressive minds. And don't give me that shit about my missing of the point: I know he is taking aim at

11

liberals, I know he is a predominately staunch Republican parading as an Independent, but liberal and progressive are not naughty words; definitely not worthy of a soapy mouth-washing. And, how about this <u>O'Reilly Factor for Kids</u>? Is this womanizing, demonizing, aggressive sermonizing William really a good influence on children? And just how much was that settlement for Bill?

Some people believe in creationism. That's funny without further expounding. Oh hell, you know I can't resist. Did you know that the earth really is flat? And the sun revolves around us while cows jump over the man on the moon. When it rains it's really God crying and lightning bolts are his way of punishing the wicked. Thunder is God fighting with that bitchy old lady of his; why do you think she got left out of the Bible? "So you think we came from monkeys mister smarty pants?" No! It was apes you stupid asshole!

Well, I suppose that's enough to make me about as appreciated as Michael Moore by our beloved leaders and blatantly biased media. I'm expecting three knocks at any time. Just remember, whatever they say about me is an outright lie. Unless it's good stuff, then it is all true. I might sound like an uber-liberal, but remember this: I support the death penalty and believe that stupidity should be adequate reason to put it to use. Let's begin with Michael Savage and Neil Bortz. Thank God for the First Amendment!

2004

A Word Play

Walk inside my world today. Let's converse through words at play: a thrilling dichotomy of all opposing parallels. Some paralysis of will, apprehension of ambition... Is superstition ruling my religion? Another childish question...

I'm a dreamer of utopian proportions. Self imposed persecution; Infliction of Auto-martyrdom; it is my birthright to create of myself a victim. Cause for a cause the lone requirement. Conspirators loot a ravaged environment. Rape!!

I scream rape in the face of liberating oppression!—A thrilling dichotomy in perpetuo moto, a gorging industry of regressive progress and mongers enforcing freedom.

Two millennia of coincidental doomsdays, and, doth the 'sooth' do as the 'sooth' say? Never did I not know the potential wasn't there for not undoing my unintentional lack of non meaningful word-dropping.

Not once never I tell you. I leave you to add up my negatives...

2004

The Passion of the Price

Why are there lines in our sky? Chemtrails form x's and poison us all. Is it to instigate the age of the beast? Is this another vanity-prone attempt to control our thoughts, to strengthen our immunity, to ready us for implants, or to create a better defense? Are they manufacturing an environment of rightful paranoia for the sake of controlling the herd? Conspiracy is more than a word, groundless and naïve; it has a basis forged in the fraud of the past. The guile of those we've elected to serve, as they spin deceit to engineer our submission. With the travesty of gaming election commissions and sub-zero standards for environmental protection, they poison our land, our water, our air. Yet the businesses don't seem to care.

In dispute with the science proving the effects of greenhouse gases, while into history our own future passes, it melts our hopes for generations to be as the glaciers meld with the seas. And they raise the level of salinity and cover the shores and devour the trees, the temperatures rise or the temperatures fall; still we have yet to see what could soon be in store. While the faithful deny this could ever even happen, they battle science to the bitter end, or until sickness or tragedy happens—then it's off to the doctor! Unfortunately, we live for the day, leaving all consequence for Hollywood to predict. I'm anticipating Arizona Bay, or as the late Bill Hicks would say, 'good riddance to the fractured egos,' or something along that order. Did somebody shout disorder?

Have you heard the ever so delightful psalm of the H.A.A.R.P? The Airforce strums it night and day, and no matter what the paid reps say, it is not for societal benefit. After all, the military represents corporate interest. But when have corporations had our safety in mind? The chiefs of staff are staining the noble profession, while charging the ionosphere with careless uncensored power in the name of protection.

Americans gorge on sour mad beef, raised in the ashes of the lush rainforests—sources of beauty and air that we breathe. I suppose a Ronald house makes up for it all, after bloating the account of the mart with the Wal. As long as we can build some more shopping malls, and always invent new holidays; commerce our god for six days...

With our president and his oil-stained soul, who surrounds himself with mere echoes, and his prince of peace with smart missiles, he'll plunder the world in control. It doesn't matter if you're from the third world or the Middle East, damage there is damage here, and filthy oceans and yellow air go great with a lab-borne disease. Corruption of our environment will march on and on as the totalitarians clinch us in their greedy green fists, while loosening restrictions on all the protection for any living thing which cannot spend. Farewell to Gaia, goodbye great spirit of earth, land and sea. You will reign again when man lies extinct.

Thanksgiving 2004

Onward All Ye Crystal Soldiers

Welcome to the new machination: a backdoor draft of the disabled and elderly, a silent draft of the uninsured and under-compensated. The Gestapo has replaced the "S" and "S" with a big fucking "W" and a greasy pseudo-smile. Bush, with all his crystal soldiers (onward all ye Christian soldiers!), has declared war on the world and rational thinking; he's become a Rove-ing lunatic—I liked him better when he was drinking. And his man Donald R., one of the few to survive in the "Chamber of Echoes" of Curious George, has sequestered the lives of the senior class, the obese, the crippled, the discharged mothers and fathers, and their children's hopes for the future. It seems all too convenient for Bush, and the appropriately named Dick, to effect stop-loss policies on today's military after dodging any real form of obligation during our country's previous engagements. Of course these men would rather defame a veteran in disgusting campaign advertisements than actually perform any acts of heroism themselves.

All of this transpires with the approval of nationalistic optimists and staunch opportunists. Salivating, sadistic, senseless, self-serving saviors of corrupt policies of conservatism, a concept contrary to progression, benefit big business with the uninformed approval of trailer park scum still steeped in the prejudices of the past, the cheerleading Religious Wrong, and the wealthy elite. Which would be the preferential liquid to purify our national pride: oil or blood? Apparently the combination works splendidly for such potential blemishes. Power to veto U.N. resolutions doesn't hurt either. Especially those dealing with the Israeli-Palestinian conflict or Iraq...

There is a frightening similitude between this caustic swaggering encroachment of value enforcement upon others, and the horrors of tragic historical consequence. And to send the weak to be slaughtered in some third world hell, or to steal the future of one person in some vainglorious attempt at delivering a future to another, is foul with the rancid odor of fallacious claims of serving divinity. Excuse me if I cannot accept the scurrilous misstatement from our 'good Christian president' that "Freedom is The Almighty's gift to mankind". Maybe 'Dubya' missed a few chapters in the inconvenient Old Testament when he formed that conviction. How does The Almighty feel about children losing their parents to avarice? How would the Lamb feel about the policy of carnivorous aggression to the detriment of his beloved children of the world?

Welcome to the new machination; a backdoor draft of the disabled, the elderly, the mothers, the fathers, the awareness of our nation's incomprehensible decline in only four years. We cannot bear to let the potential be squandered in this next term, this next trial. We must refuse to expire for corruption, for oil. America can only remain the greatest country on earth if we cease to remind ourselves, and others, of that fact. Assumption of an imperial claim to resist change and remain superior is the first step to its unraveling decay. Scream to the world, "This malfeasance has seen the end of its days!"

2004

<u>Section Two</u>

An Esoteric Predilection for the Future of Historical Fiction

Towards the Mysterium

Towards the mysterious, and then alone, transcending place, time, religion, or simply perception, will Rapture commence. A reinvention, a Rebirth, Desires Awake! We are human, Eagle, Lion, and Snake. Aloft on massive wings of bird-like grace—Creation as messiah.

And all shall be fathers of creation, mothers of inspiration. This apocalypse shall slay prejudice of the New! Lay waste to tired misconceptions, misplaced vanity and monetary corruption of our glorious art. Recognize the prophet untainted by profit. United by a cleansing ritual of emotion, Pleasure and Pain; our sadness, despair, indifference and cheer will be equally invited to the truest expression of all that we are, and ever after will strive to be.

One last time we will revel in our humanity. We will meet our end in confrontation. Not with our long, perceived enemies, but with our very selves; a vicious, raging war between conditioning and true knowledge. Fiction falls victim to Honesty! Humanity frees itself from the world, and the world from Humanity. No more subservient will, nor will to rule.

Now as gods of universes of our own, aloft on Massive, bird-like wings, and those of inspired thought. Sons of a universal philosophy, once more we are born, innocent of ignorance and unqualified judgment. Born with intuition more grand than ever was attained in the Lifetime we leave behind.

We are the Gods of universes of Inspired Will: Fathers of creation, Mothers of inspiration. All art shall be heard, all shall be seen. Every masterpiece shall be known and understood.

Mankind become animal. Become massive wave and storm! Become something more! A becoming of spirit and soul and overwhelming senses... Bring yourselves toward the Mysterium; towards the End and the Beginning. Bring All to be swallowed into All! Farewell former hindrances. Farewell dead and fallen gods of the obsolete. WE ARE THE NEW! Creation and Creator have merged.

The Mystery has been Exposed.

2003

Litmus Test for a Potential Deity

Well, I've been looking over your application and, I have to say, it is quite impressive. Before I turn you over to my colleagues for questioning, I would like to ask you some questions of my own. Do you mind submitting to a light-hearted interrogation of sorts? No? Alright then, I can see why you were nominated. It is quite refreshing to participate in the verification of such a cooperative prospective judge of mankind; this should all go rather splendidly. Being somewhat of a Letterman fan, I will stick to the format he made famous with The Top Ten Questions to Ask of a Deity Prior to Surrendering Your Common Sense and Good Fortune:

Number 1: When exactly was it that you decided you would like to sit on the vacated bench of our Supreme Being?

Number 2: Were you surprised when you received the call from the G.O.D. to fill the position, or were you already aware of the waning interest of the departing Almighty Chief Justice?

Number 3: Did you perhaps look around at the state of the earth one day and say: "You know, I think the world would be a lot better off if its inhabitants worshipped only me as their true God"?

Number 4: What do you have to offer us as followers in exchange for our obsessive devotion?

Number 5: How much self-sacrifice and aggressive witnessing would you require of said followers; or perhaps I should rephrase by asking, and this doesn't count as one of my ten questions, how much tragedy you would allow before smiting those responsible for committing violent acts in your name?

Number 6: Would you be willing to work on Sundays and show your face more than every few millennia in order to give people better access to hope, faith, and enlightenment? We had a bit of a problem with the last guy showing up and he got a real laugh out of confounding our intelligence.

Number 7: Would you be willing to relocate to other planets or solar systems if the need should arise?

Number 8: Pardon me for this next question, but you will certainly understand why I have to ask it. Would you be willing to submit some of your proverbial "holy water" for a urinalysis? Once again, your potential predecessor left mind-altering substances growing everywhere, which were responsible for hippies, black-ops and terrorist funding, and the general public's acceptance of endlessly lowered standards of entertainment and achievement, i.e., American Idol Christmas specials, Survivor, Britney Spears, Bill O'Reilly, Ann Coulter, Rush Limbaugh, fat Elvis, etc.

Number 9: Have you ever been convicted of a felony offense? For instance; homicide by the raining down of sulfur, flooding the earth to drown its inhabitants, slaying the first born of your enemies, or getting George W. Bush elected twice.

Number 10: Will your version of history contain the adorable fantasies akin to the ones we've come to know and love, like Noah's Ark, Jonah the Whale, the Virgin birth; you know, the kind of stuff that kids just go crazy for? After all, the world will be full of children after the complete ban on abortion that is about to be passed, and we need something to appease them in the absence of loving parents, health care, food, and economic stability.

I guess that is about all that I have to ask you for now. If any of the other members of this advisory board would like to actually do their job and further interview Your Omnipresent Honor, I will turn the podium over to them now. As always, I appreciate your silent candor… infinitely, Sir.

2004

The New Mythology

Step right up! Gather 'round! Let's see the last myth closing down. Very few, wary pews are open for business today. Ya see this all happened yesterday. The old time gods ran away—tired of what was done with their eminent fame, all the illness that transpired in their canonized names.

They will be remembered; by retro-pagans sorely missed. It always seems to be like this. Rise, fall, Rise, fall, My God, your god…

My eternal Father could kick your eternal Father's cloudy white ass! Quiet kids, the cycle has passed.

On and on it never ends. The new mythology might rule that bend.

Hail Mary, Praise Allah, Vishnu, see you. All over the hill I say.

The new god Cornucopia, a bit from all the former, consummate reformer—hear the skeptics sing his name.

…All just a generic form, a personified lame-man's claim.

The reality was with us from the start. I'd tell the way, but you see I haven't got the Heart.

2004

Did The Ancients Know?

Behold! I contain the secrets of God! Genetic mapping of his origins—the genuine Biblical Code…Unveil truth and deception through the piercing eyes of the Grail. Two serpents raise and ravel to form a ladder to the very heavens. A gateway to divination, to nine dimensions; the cubic third, and the solution becomes one. The all seeing holiness of knowledge: bearing the new child, the next age of confusion and realization, to cease notions of stone and systems of control—the heretical agenda of the immoral majority. An exploitation of the defenseless, of our most ominous nightmares and our greatest tragedies: truly lions.

He who would convey a message of salvation arrives in a blackened cloak of death and pestilence. The Reaper of our deepest sorrows, of our regret; inspiration for our filth, thematic abuse of our disease; Prayer to bring the Plague, bolstering of the seats of power—may this be your kind's final hour. Fall to the just reward of tainting the spiritual. Descend to the procession of hypocrisy. Verily you must be bled. The lineage of nature's enemies,

Behold! I know the secrets of God! But it is no secret that the doctrine is bathed in the blood of blasphemy. The cycle continues with the end of one trial and the introduction of perhaps another. Did the ancients ever really know?

2004

Ashes of the Thirteenth

And into view they rode. Red emblazoned crucifixes of intimidation wounding the stark whiteness of the original Nine. The fearsome holders of the Mystic Knighthood, Warriors of the Wise One's Temple, the poor men who would rise to wealth and esteem, to Masonic Legend.

Gain of power creates enemies, as former allies will attest through unflinching betrayal. The Order that need answer to none inspired jealousy and despicable want. Always the Desire for leverage precedes Inquisition. Nefarious men of judgment eager for advancement spare no mercy in the quest, their lust for blood-drenched power.

And into prominence, under the corrupted eyes of Papal deception and bankrupt nobility, they rode; opportunism and cries of heresy staining their mythology. What resemblance of justice could exist in an age of torturing the innocents—both young and old? Likewise, injustice darkened the skies with the ashes of disposable Heroes.

Friday the Thirteenth 2004

The Diminished Separation of Ignorance and Professed Morality

Lap it up, row by row—the sheep within the wolf-skin clothes. Feast on bile and convenient bibles, twisted to slander, to libel, defile.

A cautionary approach to dissenting opinions—coalition of cowering prejudiced minions. Impinge on our choice with scandalous skill. In war they rejoice: "Repent or be killed!"

Why place more value on the fetus than the living? Who will raise the children to whom life they'll be giving? That would seem an awful lot like 'playing God' to me; to cancel out conflicting wills he guaranteed to be free.

Then again, that's a premise that can never be reconciled. Freedom existing with Hell? ...A divine plan along with Belial?

They may rule the President, and absolve him of his lies. Their kind control positions of power and sacrifice our lives. Thriving on the capital gained from selling us a war, ignoring the cold reality of faltering reforms.

Forgetting that the commune had precedence with The Son—the apostles were all socialists; equal every one. They adorn themselves with the crucifix, in blasphemy reborn. They worship malice and avarice; a need for greed willingly sworn.

You can watch them on the television, or view them upon the altar, in million dollar domiciles that deny the homeless shelter. Sending out the missionaries to disrespect the varied cultures—infesting as a swarm of flies; feeding on souls like flesh-starved vultures.

A mockery of the very words they profess to hold as Truth. Deceive, believe, and bear when conceived—sigh with relief as they unleash our troops...to devastate the Heretics, the lunatics, in brave crusades that elevate the self-esteem of the flock, the herd, the fearfully saved.

Parades and games to celebrate, promised to remain celibate, as they march in pride to sanctify the loss of lives— non-Christian lives. As both sides scream out, "Infidel!" with mortar shells or Mary's hailed; they drink the blood, as if from Christ, and place the ban on new stem cells.

They've no respect for nature, for the environment: Creation. They cast aside intelligence and vote to doom all nations. The moral of this tangent, so as not to be completely misunderstood: What good are so-called moral values without the slightest semblance of ethical fortitude?

2004

Section Three

Rare Moments of Sentimentalism

I Remember Winter

I remember as a teenage boy wishing that there never was a winter's day. All of the childish joy had melted from the season along with the snowmen and angels, abandoning me to yearn only for the warmth of Spring and Summer.

Oddly enough, as a young man I began to adore the stark virginal white of the first snow preceded by the last gorgeous stand of color made by the brave trees of Fall.

One thing that I realized from all of this instability of appreciation was that change is necessary in all of Nature. It also gave solidity in concept to the old adage, "Be careful what you wish for..."

In a sad way, as my love for all seasons and my bliss at the sight of Creation's revolving dreamscape augmented, the naive wish of my teen years began to manifest itself, and Nature's variety diminished.

The chill remains. The red death and green resurrection of the Forest exist, to a lesser degree. While only a faint movement, a much labored sign of life is apparent from the seemingly comatose Opaqueness I adored as a child at Christmas. Occasionally exhibiting an awe-inspiring example of the 'Old Man's' former white might.

Currently, I am wishing for Nature's survival; a revivification of the Season's prominence. But the Mother is old and helplessly abused, suffering great malady at the hands of the plague known as Man's Arrogance.

Will the cleansing come with a miraculous cure-all? May this Creation survive to endow my children with the incomparable vision of change. Bless my end with Fall, with Frost.

2004

Of Grey and North

Contorted posture in revolving motion,

Revelatory séance of the Masters past,

Continual evolution of repertoire, ever expansive in its reinterpretation—Recomposition;

Steadfast in his will to increase the Lore, to ensure his Legend.

"So you wanna write a Fugue?"

"I dare not. But I would love to hear you perform one Glenn."

"One masterpiece comin' up…"

And so it begins:

Audible ecstasies, a shared intimacy of unabashed expression, contemplative and astute simultaneously—much like his varied late night conversations…Always the sound of unquestionable genius.

Maintaining an air of supremacy coinciding with kind immediacy, sharp cynicism balanced with good-hearted wit and charm. Puritan and artist converge in unified endearing eccentricity.

Psychosomatic self-diagnosis of illness borne of the proposed cure, of a maternal veil of sheltered security; the world locked outside of his inner imposed surreality. Hypochondriacal loner of virtuosic proportions…Every aspect of his life as extremely unique as the gifts he was given with which to succeed. To excel in all individual pursuits, while failing only in human relationships and interaction.

Despiser of Romantic Decadence,

A colorful personality submerged in f minor and grey. Tinted wool solitaire, symbolic of the North, of Nature and its true endowment of prodigious talent…Then a fatal Stroke...

Just to hear those first few bars of the Goldberg Aria at the hands of Gould. That is knowing the reality of inexplicable Brilliance.

2004

In memory of Glenn Gould 1932-1982

A Passage for Zoe

Graciously grant me forgiveness for utopia lies in your eyes,
…Blue as waves on pristine oceans reflecting magnificent skies.
A blessing of Angelic beauty, Enchantment brushed a smile upon your face;
A masterwork of sheer benevolence, a masterpiece of innocent grace.
Your laughter elates my very spirit—A Choral Symphony;
The chorus of divine creation in resounding euphony.
Year by year, with the passing of time, only your growth parallels my fatherly pride,
For all that you are and all you become, I pledge myself to stand by your side.
I pray the passage of Zoe is blessed with immeasurable fulfillment and cheer.
May your heart know love, may your body know strength,
May your mind know all, may your soul resist fear.
Graciously grant my forgiveness, if ever I fail you, when my life is no more.
I will find you through eternity; with infinite wings of unity—
Together again we will higher soar.

2004

Unveil a Fathomless Consciousness

Lull me, lull me ever deep. Deep like thought's caress of dream. Alto wings, soprano screams, Coltrane cries, Tyner swings.

And Garrison pour your heart too low, through sweat, through tears, conjoined to Jones.

Unveil a fathomless consciousness: unravel and entwine— architecture through confinement's demise. Crush to build. Smash! Create!

Prejudice, pride, angst, spite, exorcise, fade, eradicate: a revelation, an inspiration— supreme and spiritual— intense, yet sentimental.

A modern Musical Offering. Shhhhh...Listen...The voice of God? His transcendental choir of beauty and violence, Intensity! Supremacy! Listen.

12 pitches to unveil a new book of John. 20th century Bach? No, just 'Trane.

A divine quest of paragon invention; blue etudes beyond a collective conscience deify the mood. Representatives of courageous insight.

Not much time and a memory became life. These words mean absolutely nothing. Shhhhh...Listen! Omniscient, omnipotent, omnipresent—that sound you hear is legacy.

2002

Negligence

The Angels held your hand last night, as life granted you a passing kiss. A loving spirit by pain's weight crushed, or elevated will to exist?

Watering eyes shall grieve you no more, for selfishness pleases no soul. Harmonious sound of our voices engaged, exalting in diminished control.

An ingrate was I to take you for granted—one so precious faced neglect. The passing of time is man's Anathema; too immeasurably short to reflect.

Upon circumstance that cannot be undone, shameful relations abound. A pathetic state of remorse-bred slumber; Inescapable misery surrounds.

Your loss a knife that makes my heart bleed. My spirit grown cold can serve not to lead.

Never again to stand inspired by your strength; in awe filled contemplation my faith lies extinct.

A trifling life of solitary chains, the bindings of a mechanized rebirth, a portrayal of apprehension that suits you well, neither here or away from this earth.

Is it greed that I grieve? Can pity succumb to need? Nurturing selfishness and sewing complacent seeds. My life is void, and in a sense, my soul has passed away with you; a twisted ploy—but could fate reunite me with you?

1996

Awake and Dreaming

Am I awake, alas, to a chorus of light? Cherub sung beauty harkens audible tears.

Euphonious clarity, a new breath of life; brought down to kneel, drained of my cheer.

You see, the Siren have sung of my doom. They carry my soul to a glorious ruin.

Ensnared! Enraptured! I must see this through! Defiant of Fate that keeps me from you.

And who could it be that urges me on? I have yet to know. Still yet I long.

I long for the truth, I long for her love to save me from hell, to bring me above.

To remove all my anger, to banish my pain, though thus far in life it seems so in vain.

I will prevail, through all, I proceed. To regain my hope is the one thing I'll need.

1996

To Watch the Moon Rise

"I'm going up on the mountain to watch the moon rise." I remember those days, I treasure those times.

A small, curious and adoring shadow I was even then, striving to be as you were, as you are, and always have been.

You are the penultimate example of understanding, caring, love, respect and strength; all of this then, now and evermore—your strength of body, mind, and spirit an absolute beacon of light and truth.

Did we ever see that moon rise, Grandpa? Have we scaled that mountain of late? Were we ever truly away?

Was that mountain life, the moon a metaphor for aspiration, the innocent beginnings of a lifetime of inspiration, of encouragement and pride instilled throughout our times? Together, or apart, whether near or even far—nothing could take this memory away.

Morning sun upon the garden, you are there, I am there. This is no dream, no recollection. Always we are there—a great man and his ever adoring shadow.

2003

Come the Dawn

The evening has arrived—that uninvited guest of twilight, of mourning the long lost morning;

This descent into a deep blue midnight, a violet hue, my thoughts ever of you.

How cold it seems without your enveloping touch—falling into a desperate battle against fear and uncertainty.

I parallel a lonely Autumn moon, obscured by the bitter cold clouds of fast approaching Winter. What beckons this nocturne desperation, owed to my angel, my all, my inspiration?

Why are these words falling as leaden tears? I feel such joy when we are together, as to lay shade upon my heart when we are apart. Ah yes, love…no tremendous insight needed to assess my momentary affliction. The cure will arrive with a new day—my reunion with you— only you, ever after, forever more.

Come the dawn—bring closure to this needless insecurity, burn through my hesitant, forced slumber. Awaken me to a new day's hope. Come deeper within my soul with your spirit's illumination. Bring closure to this prolonged evening of bitterness and despair.

This is destiny blessed by fate—too real for chance or circumstance. From the very moment I met you it was apparent. No, we never really met at all did we? Our souls, our very hearts, were merely reconciled, relinquished from want and need, carried from valleys of loneliness and shadows of doubt, delivered into beautiful union, as if by the hands of a true divinity.

We cannot allow this to end in regret. It must be, for it is meant to be. Who could deny such truth, such happiness? No separation for bonds young, yet inseparable. Very few empty evenings remain. Soon our lives will be together as one.

For now, I slip into unconsciousness and dream only of you. Our future awaits. Come the dawn, come the dawn.

2003

Of Great Men

Hail to my brothers of earthly enlightenment: Fathers of the theoretical, Mothers of invention (yes, those Mothers...). All of those bent on achievement. Rediscover the origin. Past and present revisited and visited.

The future shown by a man in France, another view by one named Edgar—he the healer, the seer, "There is a river", The Sleeping Prophet.

Christ, The Buddha, Muhammad—all great men; the unfortunate victims of misinterpretation. Another J. C. taught us the Light we carry within.

Much to the chagrin of Ptolemy, along came Copernicus, Galileo, Einstein and Hawking. Relativity evolves to the Super String.

From the contrapuntal elaborations of Bach in reverence to God to the playing of paintings and the liberation of dissonance; Music ushers in Revolution—the poetry to bear the Mysterium.

A wash of colors: Realistic, Surrealistic, Form, shape, shade and light; Leonardo, Bacon, Picasso, prior and beyond. Spearhead the movement of the current foresight.

The incredible power of words: Philosophy to bring empowerment, a Fictional Zarathustra. Schopenhauer at opposition with Kant...overly embellished, stylistic movements that lead and follow, lead and follow... with Bosquet, Rimbaud, Baudelaire, Blake, Joyce, Waugh and Kafka to illuminate.

So many great men have come before us. More than any amount of words, any dedication of sentiment, can ever mention.

No tome could begin to comprise.

No slight could ever compromise

The achievement, the endowment,

The veritable infinity of progress:

The percipience of our intellectual predecessors...

2004

Section Four

Schizophrenia Can Be a Liberating Experience for a Would-Be Philosopher

The Birth and End of Corruption

If there is anything that has become increasingly apparent in the new millennia, it is that those in power are as self-serving as they have ever been; be they political or religious leaders, or heads of corporations. Power is the source of far more corruption than the most incredible wealth conceivable, although the two at some point inevitably coincide. These are the dual roots of all evil, if I might borrow a tired phrase. There is of course a third root of all evil, and that is man. In fact, I will go so far as to state the shamefully obvious fact that, without man, there would be no corruption.

Man, in all of his inherent pride, invented the concepts of wealth and power to establish dominance over one another often times inconsistent with the Darwinian theory of survival of the fittest. With the establishment of concepts such as value, debt, and servitude, in contrast to abundance, wealth, and nobility, our modern social travesty emerged. Add to that the manipulations, so easily manifested through man's fear, which religious sects have preyed upon from their very inception; and the plot of mankind's self-inflicted enslavement thickens.

Through politics, belief systems and corporate cunning, there is perpetuated a competitiveness that is detrimental beyond compare to the fabric of potential unity. These separate entities have learned from history well enough to know an all-important lesson: that man's insecurity is essential for control. Nationalism, materialism, racism, chauvinism, feminism, reverse-racism, political affiliation, religious affiliation, etc., etc., on and on: man-made division is carried out through excess segregation.

Power in the hands of a very few has the potential for tragic consequence. Decisions of national and international importance should be made without the corrupting influences of religious endorsements and corporate donations. A variety of opinions and the ability, if at all possible, to compromise ideology to spare lives and the environment, should prevail at the highest levels of all nations. This type of reasoning is considered weak by those in positions of abundant power, but it would be wise to remember that pride has been the downfall of many an empire.

Every country should be defined by the will of the majority of its people; indifferent to the amount of wealth they have acquired. However, freedom and equality are the responsibility of the oppressed to demand, not a gift to be given at the expense of their lives. If people are to die for freedom, let it be in a revolution of their own choosing.

There might come a day when the people of all nations stand in defiance of the familial generations of power-brokers—the modern and future nobility—and demand that unity is essential for any long term survival; that incessant wars are barring our further evolution; that religion should enlighten and strengthen our ability to accept differences of faith in brotherhood, or in turn, be relinquished of its sway over humanity and seen as a failed invention that has outlived its usefulness; that corporations would uphold some code of ethics and be held accountable for pollution and corruption; in short, that power would become a responsibility and shared blessing for humanity and our environment.

Our will cannot eternally submit to 'the way things are', or to any abstract source of oppression. Reason should never be enslaved by fear or any selfish ideal of materialism. Let the ancient mistake of inequality go the way of all things ancient—into history and out of whatever present time it has afflicted. Let judgment be made through knowledgeable consideration and individual actions, as prejudice and intimidation of any kind fades away.

2004

<u>They Said</u>

They say the pen is mightier than the sword, but what I've always wanted to know is who the hell are they?

At least in this case they're revealed to be thieves of Bulwer-Lytton's credit…

These anonymous, opinionated purveyors of ill-fated decision making never seem to be around during the incessant 'They' name-dropping.

Sometimes I am forced to ask myself, "Do 'they' even exist beyond their verbal perpetuation?"

The fault always rests with them, and by them I mean 'they'.

"They said this movie was great."

"They are taking our jobs."

"Oh, but they said this was an excellent restaurant."

Do you see what I mean? A lifetime of decision making hangs in the balance of a second person review.

Variations on a Theme of 'They'…

I will tell you one thing in summation, and I'm sure that 'they' would concur—Never Bring a Pen into a Sword Fight!

2004

Scapegoat

Beware, beware the evildoer; he who dares to be his own—to hold his own ideal, to have his own ideas, to follow only those whom he truly may revere.

Not the same as all the others, the Blackest of his brothers. Who is he to propagate such Heresy, such honesty? What is he? Where is he? Everywhere and in all things: The Eternal Excuse.

The holder of blame and flame for all shameful actions, whatever we do that could expose the genetic flaw bred into us all. Each society contains this Aberration. He who was the Benefactor morphed into The Accuser, but might return to prominence someday.   Or so it was written, but has yet to be done. Hell perhaps lies deep within the Sun.

The Eternal Prometheus– ever giving us warmth and cancer, giving light to our lives or burning them to black ash; always black in the end. Darkness equates danger and sin.

And always The Fall: from the garden, from the heavens, from every beneficial grace; women and wolves and signs of the serpent, all ill-accused, stripped of all trace of virtue or propriety.

Decry the lie, the duplicity, the treachery: a lineage of denial, a boundless displacement of guilt and its acceptance—another devil to soothe the wound of conscience and empathy. Beware that deviation. Cast out demons! Personality cancelled. Find someone to blame. Always misplace the blame.

2004

The Jung and the Zealots

There is a farce we have in common: the inability to see 'good' due to an all consuming quest to expose evil. Can you believe we have common ground? Does that sicken your insides as it does mine; thus proving the incendiary initial point?

The Jungian theory: so insidious a plot of evolution or God. Streaming unified consciousness equals an odd form of self loathing, don't ya think? I never expected that you did. But don't be insulted, if we are one I insult also me. Or I? Myself is running away from such nonsense as you would expect from an Oedipal Freudian bastard like him. It's all rather confusing isn't it?

Damned mind quacks and their pompous cigars—phallic symbols of authority; to hell with the couch trip, acid trip, or round trip. I'm outta here, and sticking it out with my previous disgust of (y)our kind.

2004

Speak Enslavement's Will

Will the truth ever be revealed in classes with dated books? Learn the past well, or a new century repeats. A life summed up in days, like short and pointless stories. Fools and mortality parted as seas in ancient myth.

Are there any takers—a ticket to 'the end'? Let's get the trip over with; we'll fall right off of the edge. Existence again is lost with a toothy smile. Animate puppets speak enslavement's will. Wave on the way down, until we meet again; leave your audience speechless. But who's controlling whom?

1995

James Christopher Pitts

Beyond the Veil of Perception

One can never really solve the mysterious stratagem of time; the spasmodic and evasive prognosis of the fourth dimension. Relativity seems somewhat of a misnomer when dealing with the erratic behavior of this measured influence—simultaneously predictable and inconceivably perplexing. The nebulous providence of a moment that passes the very instant it comes to be. And the old adage that 'time waits for no man' stands remarkably true, while I can assure you that it never 'stands still'.

Our only escape from these ageless conditions is to shatter the veil of perception, transcending the illusion of a singular universe to discover the hypnotic allure of dissimulation. The revelation of our willingness to accept invisible boundaries, to honor that which has no tangible evidence beyond the waning beauty of us and our surroundings would then be apparent. However, the degeneration of our health, the rotation of that searing deity of approbation with its setting and blazing rebirth, the rust and rot of our material belongings, our children's progress as they surpass us in strength and capability, our own regression to incapacity and infantile vulnerability: these are imposing reassurances of the march of time.

What would happen if time was given no ponderous acknowledgement? A fresh approach to the proverbial tree falling in the woods with equally disappointing results; the tree would still fall and we would still grow old and die. The bodily outcome might never be altered, but the veil of perception as we know it would cease to be. The first step to the bridging of dimensions, of space, and of universes within equidistant reach—even endlessly entwined, would have finally been taken. Ignorant of the long established limitations imposed by keeping with the conduct of our age, life would bear the fruit of refreshing satisfaction and a new understanding of freedom. Alleviation of this obstacle which seems beyond our control would be the giant leap to carry mankind to a new reality; boundlessly we would pierce the mirror of consciousness, bending the last fragments of space-time to discover our many selves in the innumerable worlds of the former void. Time would truly remain forever 'present'.

2004

In Order To Be Human

As I reflect upon the words I have written of late, I sense a definite abundance of haughty conclusion.

Sickeningly dogmatic, yet symptomatic of my cage-like surroundings, my utter chagrin with the state that we're in.

Seems I'm at it once again: rebukes, reprimands, and stern reprobation, as if I know it all, as if I hold the answers.

Why the fuck do you think I ask so many questions?

And, why all of this rhyme, but rarely a reason; using alliteration allocation, alluding to my altered treason?

And then I say you, or they, or we; to flee from the sole responsibility of statements that sodomize decent sensibility, and if I rhyme once more I'll just damn well scream!

I began these words with an issue in mind, aside from a much needed bout with self-effacing.

The exposure of my opprobrium was certainly to have a grand scheme; we've come much too far for me to be all-the-sudden self-deprecating.

The point to be made might be viewed askew, might be seen polemic, will lack obeisance and divine quintessence, once more I will be the Body's sarcoma, while keeping my ass off the tower.

As best as I can I'll avoid the soap box, if you believe that then you must get your news from Fox.

That's a tad bit too gullible to do anyone good, please steer clear of the polls…

To err is human, to realize it, well, um, that's also human. There will be no pathetic awards today just for behaving as we should anyway.

Some say Christ was the only human to meet perfection, but humans don't perform any resurrections, and men have desires and endless erections—where was all of that in the book?

What of this Mary and those nasty rumors? A harlot among men makes sense to me, and might even prove Jesus' humanity.

No sacrilege intended you know my intent is pure, I just want to establish the motive.

To be God's son and also God, and last mere hours upon the cross, it's all just not adding up.

If Christ had lived the life of man, without having certainty to the end, perhaps I could begin to understand.

Nevertheless, the claims just don't ring true, you can't have a God and human too, that can't be right, that can't be fair.

I am man and bound to err.

I'll admit right now that within I'm dark; I'm sin, I'm pain, and fear with heart.

Contorted by the life I would die to protect: that's what it takes to be human.

2004

Section Five

The Perdition Testimony or Things Better Left Unsaid

The Question Found Answers Tonight

How does it make you feel when my stare burns into your soul, do you sense that I await you? In shadows the veil of innocence torn to shreds; I emerge to claim what is mine. Without mercy: forgiveness found only through bloodshed, vengeance and tears.

A jagged caress of the paleness, ecstasy and fright melt together with flesh. And I witness within your panic lies pleasure—beyond those astonished, wide glassy eyes as you lie there broken and take me inside.

No more pedestal! No careless, blind reverie. Nevermore the idolatry, the worship you never deserved. A waste, was it all—your life, our love? …Your pretension of knowledge, or lack thereof? A waste of respect and useless regret… Swiftly ends the sentence. The Question found answers tonight.

In these waning moments finality begets more wonder. Did you wake in a state of apprehension? …A precognitive trance, a premonition? Hell rests assured premeditation was born as you left me behind.

Betrayal is the ultimate insult, the deepest inspiration for a backlash of judgment. And the hand of Judgment is cold and cruel to the deceitful lust of your kind.

Remember the last promise you gave to me, only to cover the sickening truth of your nature? Well, guess the promise I swore to myself as I saw deception straight through your eyes. There is probably not a hint of recollection. Not a goddamned clue in your shallow mentality why such harm would come at my hands. Only your own petty existence, your material senseless want, has ever been clear to you.

So many questions, so much doubt and insecurity—don't you dare plead! Don't fucking beg mercy from me! Where was my relief from agony; my release from torment? Torment that no perdition, no putrid hell, could ever exceed.

Must you really ask why I withdrew? Went deep within? Why now? As you fade away you develop a conscience? Don't waste your last gasping breaths feigning concern for my suffering. I'll whisper you a poem full of answers to lull you on to nothingness; of spite a gift from trust. Pain presented as love. And love a word that brims with insincerity: a facade, a charade, a gleeful fucking calamity—wielded with absolute belligerence upon a once great and affectionate soul.

Now you lie there so weak and pathetic, just a few more moments of togetherness—an intimate finale' between old friends. Look into my eyes, the proverbial mirror, a reflection from absolute depth. Do you see your falsehood, your pitiful decline? You are pestilence but immediate eradication would prove far too kind. Dwell on the filth that you have always been inside.

Are you now able to comprehend the necessity of your fall; how your end will benefit myself, one, and all? Breathe the final affirmation. The question found answers tonight.

2002

A Few Dreary Days

In just three short days grace has completely withered, and this spiraling decline of relations transpired in unison with Nature's rebirth—a bitter preparation for a 'Black Easter' and a 'Bad Friday' (if you will and if I might)...

No reconciliation foreseen; no second comings in these few dreary days—devoid of the chance for a divine resurrection. No saviour of age old lore to flee the condemning tomb we have made for ourselves.

...Only one Last Supper; and that leaving a blackened cavity deep within my chest.

Why the betrayal? What humanity was there to save from itself this time; with you playing multiple roles of Mary, Veronica, Judas and Pilate? Kiss the cheek, wipe the blood, and drive the fucking nails ever deeper! No virgin birth from those tentacles of your womb, thrice torn and ravaged; and for what?

How did the denial of your faults grow to such immeasurable dimensions; so convinced of your own righteousness that no prostitution of your soul is self revealed?

Now the revelation of identity is known, and you, I, the two of us: the beasts of eyes, of horns, of servitude. How are we the plague, as well as its victims? This schizophrenic faith will not allow growth, a necessity in my mind while a vile sin to your suffocated outlook.

So here is the end, the parting of fiction-based bonds of loyalty, the split of two confused and confusing spirits of neglect. How the trust tears and rips, bleeding like so many deflowered innocents.

An unimaginable schism formed in mere hours, with us standing at opposing sides. However, there is an immense towering cliff, and a choice to scale it and overcome or collapse in intimidation and seclusion.

I will move beyond this obstacle, but what of you? Will you ever break your pursed lips away from the bloated breast of dependency? Are you to continue on the dark path of insecurity veiled by transparent faith; always trapped in the labyrinth of your pettiness, your selfishness, and plain stupidity? No, there will be no reincarnation of our spirits united; no rapture for two damned and heartless shadows.

But in this eternal refusal I incessantly grow. Even as we are dust, withered and dried up—taken by the wind. This, our Black Easter, Our Bad Friday... My freedom came in three short dreary days, but what of yours?

Easter Weekend 2003

The Adoration of Infliction

Oh, tell me it is not you again, arrived to reap vengeance upon the holder of your flame—a vengeance greater than the epitome of callous hatred. One inspired by the truest love to lay shade over my kingdom. Abstract in form, yet radiant despite, stand the Angels with whom eternal reckoning has become my deepest fear and desire.

Unclear is my sight for it is blurred by tears and adoration; smitten by respectful intimidation—afraid for my faltering sanity— drawn by the quartering horses of your emotions and pulled into despair, hope, affection and rejection; the Opposers of stable reality.

1995

<u>The Edge</u>

I lie teetering…I measure the fall, as the rungs of my ladder crash with the wall.

Why all these echoes, that sound not at all like mine; whispering calls, through the halls of splintering pine.

"Who is that?"

"Why is he here?"

"What could it be?"

"Why do I fear?"

"Is he my conscience, a spirit divine, a being of light traveling time?"

No, I am pain; I am faith once it's crushed. I am bitterness and torment— the pillars of Lust. This the beginning, for never it ends: the blessing, the burden, as if birth were my sin.

2000

__Not of Bathory__

Blindly strayed with angelic wings, mocking strides of Choral rings;

Bathe me gently Elizabeth. Wrung and distraught, vindictive songstress.

Vitality doused with acidic lust. Wrath of the wench—condescendence a must.

Achievement of climax through hurt you inflict. Another has stained you, may vengeance be swift.

These eyes have filled rivers and oceans alike. Naught has come of this, save her delight.

Weariness brought me to lie with the devil: the venomous queen of original evil.

Arouse my suspicion, emotion and shame. Endow the evangels the gift of its name.

Identity known, 'tis this sleek, brittle creature; a wickedly sly and whoring deceiver.

1996

Sardonic and Vague

Eyes melting, molten endearment, the trustee caressed by flirtatious blades—a rusting red embrace.

Grieve the gracious, solvents mingle; a strychnine honey of derisive dosage.

How does one endure this illusion of chance, with its poison tipped arrows of cathartic intent?

Pierce and enlighten the opportunist. Cleanse the proclaimers of purity, of poise. Eternal borrowers: life-force lusting, suckling darlings.

Fate spitting acid in guise of redemption…is it but for attention? Absolute nonsense!

Return my kingdom dominatrix! Unhand the claim of inflated genius—flammable flags of Narcissus' dreamland.

Let the stolen hopes burn in pyromantic fantasy lest the fake reclaim them.

May their wretched, filth clad, delusional arrogance be met with an army of malicious self-degradations.

2000

Lamentation

Lamentation fades, are you sad to see it go, as ice chipped away by blazing summer sun?

And with it burns our patience—a blessing, but from whom? Admire the unattainable, lay before their vile path, to trample the adoring peon to dust, or strip away this layer of trust? Oh, the joy so beyond measure. With each bruise a flower, with each teardrop sprout glorious trees, each droplet a sanguine sea—thus a world of torture to tease.

Hail the few to care-a-less, they alone just might survive; to tell the youth there is no treason—the elusive illusion their only friend.

Their loving neighbors: bitter seeds. Their mother's arms: smothering weeds. Father's warnings: a vicious trap, Brothers and sisters with bleeding backs.

This is doctrine, our heritage, our pride? When we fight in name of honor we feed our conscience lies.

2000

Say What Thou Wilt Shall Be the Role of In-laws

Her mouth is open wide to reveal a tongue that forks, and roams among a row of fangs to form raw words as truth contorts. An off-putting display of rancid opinion, malformed intention, and character assassination, through maternal dominion spewed with the fervor of a mental reformer: a priestess—mock preacher; but who would believe her?

How about the so-called friends of the one I love, most above, who lost her dreams of a wedding day surrounded by those she held dear. I watched my wife's spirit carry the weight of disappointment, of unfortunate guilt, I watched my wife grow to a woman that day with strength, resolution and the blessing of will.

Perhaps I've been too harsh with stooping to her mother's level, perchance I stand in common pulpits banging ignorance' gavel. And maybe she just wants the best for her beloved son or daughters, and there'll never be anyone good enough to take her place, or their father's. But, then again, we've never met and yet the trash compounds: bad man, bad father, drug abuser, woman user, non-Christian, occult religion, New Age believer, satanic deceiver—the web of lies spins 'round and 'round.

And then there is the 'head of house', although mom still wears the pants, who wouldn't look into my eyes to measure up the man I am. Still he found the time to seek the answers I could have told him. And with a weak investigation, based on presumptive fabrication, his case only further yet emboldened: bad man, bad father, drug abuser, woman user, non-Christian, rock musician, liquor swiller, serial killer…He wouldn't look me in my eyes, but still he spewed malignant lies, while screaming for the blood of Christ to wash my filth away. And he damned me for my divorce of course, and cast aside reason's discourse, and denied my path to Heaven's gate as if I was a leper, as if I were gay.

The day we met I knew the truth behind his seeming shyness. What he tried to hide inside was blatantly obvious, the eyes never lie. I read the disapproving gestures, spread open as if from a book, I knew that he had formed his prejudice before we had words, averting his look.

"…Not very inconspicuous with your feelings dear sir or Dad if you'll humor me…No?"

"Never!"

Approval means nothing in the light of a rush to assumption. Absolution must be earned for these transgressions. However, they're much too proud to apologize; kidding aside, what's the Bible say of pride?

And as much as these right wing, Savage-scene, warriors of Christ read the Word, to question their knowledge would just be absurd. Especially by a completely un-ethical filthy liberal who they couldn't relate to as I'm less hypocritical, who married their daughter without their consent, less their approval or close to a blessing. And I haven't spent much time on my knees confessing; or for that matter very much else. But I assure them I'm not sent from hell. And I don't hold others to standards I could never achieve—like abstinence and joy, and a choice to conceive. I don't place on her immeasurable guilt or self conscious fear of reprobation unreal. And her happiness isn't based upon impossible laws, or humanity's flaws that were never her fault. I do apologize for the sting of my honesty with regards to her parents and their dire misguidance, I'm sorry for the forked tongue comment that seemed a bit childish. But, at least there are a few things for me to rectify now, as I'd hate our shared humanity to be overlooked or left out.

Now, in closing this engrossing tale of mistreatment it remains instrumental—to remind that any similarity to actual events is completely coincidental.

Thanksgiving Day 2004

Section Six

Arcane Lyrical Evidence of the Infamous Students of Alchemy

The Next Step

Spiraling regression: I Reflect upon the past to face the future… Direction: lost in a puzzling lapse of judgment…Confusion: slips deep into my consciousness, pulling me so much further than reason could ever withstand.

My vision roaming through sound as I listen to vivid colors, Juxtaposing fragments for the sake of the greater whole.

Devouring information, facts to fuel the creative wars, in turn, will give way to advancements unimaginable. Beyond: Beyond the limits of Universe and Time. Left behind are the false concepts of Infinity/Eternity; looking down upon the waning gods, impious, a truly omnipotent view.

Birth of a new Hierarchy that will outlast the brilliance of the stars—there are those who speak against this prophecy.

What filth!! What will their meager words mean when they become the habitat of worms? Caverns in which the vermin shall play and procreate, this is their lone purpose at last.

No, their criticisms mean little as this testimony manifests. Generation after generation my name is ever more Empowered.

Beyond I say! Shall the echoes of greatness bring about avalanches to ever silence the Opposers of this testament—those baneful, lecherous children of Servitude. This evolution has already begun. Unbeknownst, they will stagnate in their satisfactory non-existence.

What began as near breakdown has produced revelation. …A flirting bout with Insanity? Or waking to grand realizations? I have gained so much more than I ever could have lost. Do not judge me wearied or weak, I'm psychologically beyond reproach.

What is gone from me was expendable, merely the last aspects of Humanity, of guilt, morality. All traces gone! Beware the dawn! For the next evolution has already begun.

(Featured on Scholomance - The Immortality Murder cd 2002)

Virus: The Theft of Knowledge

Gather my children, grant heed the elder. Time will now pass its wisdom down. All must cease, to take in this splendor. Script foreseen shall come to be.

Call on the winds; we ride with the Tempest to distant stars questing for truth, to spread like a plague, with knowledge our Virus; Infecting Oppression while stealing back our lives.

Shattered chains no longer bind that which gives our culture life. In rebirth our minds thrive. These strengths increase with passing time.

Deliver us beyond the seas, to lay foot on shores of never Dawn. Silhouettes of dusk-drawn trees, screaming hymns to brothers lost.

Endless rain can not wash away the traces of Heaven, born of Earth, we forsake.

Omniscience a shadow cast goal, desires aflame cannot be quenched. Enlighten us, The Bondage Estranged, ever parched for proof and reason. Monuments cannot please need. To none shall we bow or lend endowment. A lust which cannot be conceived will not bend or sway beneath ignorance.

Strive to know, to recognize, progression. Defiant of the Burden faced in Man's retrogression.

Call on the winds; we ride with the Tempest to distant stars questing for Truth. To spread like a plague, with knowledge our Virus, Infecting Oppression while stealing back our lives.

(Featured on Scholomance – The Immortality Murder 2002)

The Mathematics of Divinity

Our preprogrammed laughter and screams hint at a divine insanity.

Slithering Saints in grand corridors, Whores bent upon "God-fearing" knees.

Torturous, writhing figures emerge,
From ivory cast icons they surge,
To tear the last shreds of decency,
To conjure up shrouds of infamy…

The righteous must fall, tyrants them all; an eternally flawed misconception to perpetuate our misdirection.

In the beginning a slave was created, next came judgment and fear. …Examples of time and communication, minimal knowledge and limited years. This creature, forged to serve the necessity of his creator—the ultimate goal. A certain degree of naivety and an innate will to be controlled.

"Oh this yearning, the insatiable need."

"Am I abandoned, alone?"

"All of these trials I have yet to face."

"What if I am unable to go on?"

"To continue without you would condemn forever my soul."

"To remain unfulfilled, empty inside, denied this desire for the truth to be shown."

In the beginning, were we a creation? Could omniscience allow such mistakes? Or, was evolution tampered with to increase or moderate? Was belief intrinsically linked to need, through process of forceful submissive response? Is imagination implanted, or anomaly? Can humans truly have inspired thought?

"I renounce all judgment! I renounce blind faith! Because my thoughts are only mine and I control my Fate."

"The shackles are as dust, and I in time will be. But I'll curse you all before I fall, and Rule my destiny!"

In the beginning…what beginning?! The infinite a concept that humans cannot comprehend… To measure in relation to a miniscule mortality what is unbounded and knows no end. There are mysteries, numeric parallels, and clues to render useless all that once was God; or perhaps to confirm an origin, of manipulation from distant stars.

"Oh, this yearning, this insatiable need."
"I am abandoned alone…"
"And all of these trials, orphaned I face."
"I must overcome and move on!"
"To continue without you has condemned
forever my soul."
"I'll find fulfillment within myself."
"You denied my desire for all of the truths to be shown."

A trace of Orion is shown in History clear. Those who control us: Genetics, Genesis, Fear…

2001

What Was Truth

"My disgust commences at the end of what was truth." This doctrine of hollow promises would cease mortality. Faith in vain rewards regret, take to heart this crime of fraudulent documentation to moralize mankind. The posthumous foresee an end to parasitic rule.

We, though few, will wage the war to destroy this barbarism; towering in such egoism as to reach beyond the heavens. With brevity and fact as will, we will "crush idols with philosophy's hammer."

Contempt—our deity Power— principled liars mute knowledge and culture. "I prefer to question rather than accept." ...A forbidden yearning for absolute science. A god excused by non-existence grants no pardon when we take reign.

With just our presence the silent masses roar, audible with conviction's authority. A labyrinth of predestination—end of contagious suffering. No pity for those pitied, reclaim our throne of nature. With this battle for order under way, we will leave morality defamed upon its cross.

"Need no Christian charity." Be superior in thought. Need no hope, 'evil of evils', conceptualize destiny as god. Follow now with Pilate; leave the 'Wandering Jew'. Revaluate all values— strength restored through wounds.

(I was heavily under the influence of Nietzsche at the time of this writing, making this a bit more of an atheistic piece of piracy/dedication not entirely in agreement with much of my current philosophy. I do however adore the man for his courage, talent and genius as much as the first moment I discovered him—his words are an elegant liberation for the damned. Quotations from several of his books were used liberally and credited to the best of my memory's ability with quotation marks. Lyrics were featured on Scholomance - A Treatise on Love cd 1997.)

Pride of the Serpent Winds

I scorch these plains; I wield the crown of the Apocalypse. Burning through what once was you to free my yearning soul. Yet, with this seal, seventh past, my head is lowered still. Ashamed by waste you have left behind with careless indulgence

So draw the swords, four at once, hope is banished all. Loose the cries on desert winds to wash this ash away. Serpents sway with glee now, this final charming call. Gain their trust, then strike with vengeance; befriend them as they fall.

The venom is coursing through their bodies, weak and frail, now gone. But spirits rise to scream once more, "Afterlife has come!"

A failed decree to crush the free wanderers of the barren dune; they will always stand—passion's strength may earn my empathy.

Respect the valor, though foolish pride, to face my blade of plague. Bleeding honor stains the sands which scatter vanity.

Desperation utters forth soft whimpers. Power has lost the meaning derived. I refuse to spare this selfish breed, with its indecency and hollowed remains.

Visionary men and gods are proven false—Warriors are slaves shed of bindings. Populace has freed us to reign—Mounting our steeds we continue on...

...To spread heavenly carnage across this rumored holy land.

Praise wasting dreamers cower on sight, of Christ In retreat to spare his second life.

(Featured on Scholomance - A Treatise On Love cd 1997.)

65

I Am That Which Is

What peril in this grievous testament? Fate, in its mischievous irony, has cruelly toppled my health. Why creator, why deprive me of the most joyous of senses?

I, godlike among men in both art and thought; sensitivity drains upon this misunderstanding—mine and theirs. To view Nature is truly to look upon the inevitable

All might be well tomorrow, that is the great wish. That it has or ever will be granted: blind illusion.

Albeit, aloneness is the prize of genius—Passions attained would cause songs to become silent.

And so, I am heir to bereavement, threnody is my mistress alas. It must be, yet the muse embraces me—her warm heart to stoke this inner flame.

And drown out the mortals and petty theology with heroic composition!

I'll not suffer the scars of kindred feelings—Allowing this lowly world to aggravate me momentarily—Only to escape to my melodic bliss––creativity thrives… in bitterness.

My veil is untouchable, talent unattainable—I Am That Which Is, love loss and scorn—left to bleed through hammered counterpoint.

Indulge my vast ambition—defy horrific fates. Banished from a poisoned life to shadows; a looming backdrop to the paintings of our lives

No tears shall fall from hushed eyes—Glints of splendor, Lovelorn cries. Gather the drops that they may cease to sink, deny the Earth of that addictive drink.

With years adoration will simply grow. I'll reach their worship from funereal woe.

…Never attained an equal release, to my melancholic masterpiece.

(Dedicated to the memory of Ludwig van Beethoven, with a few quotes from the maestro and friends. Featured on Scholomance – A Treatise on Love cd 1997)

Light Defiance

The living have never seen me. Those dead I guess they might… have seen these feasting eyes upon them, with teeth of red tinged white. Hide away the cherub for youthful blood is life. As zephyr blows, to chill the soul, resurrection comes at night. My lust is like a universe far beyond sight, far beyond heaven's reach yet spilling forth with life. A leeching fiend, how I am enthralled by venesection, bred of purest lineage; dragons symbolize my cognation.

Blasphemy has bore me to feed its hunger; parched and more ravenous with less desire to wander. I remember my creator being cast into the sun. By members of our own commune: I destroyed every one. How his flesh defied the light, but slowly fell to ash; a martyr for lost centuries—now his kind has passed.

Grasp at desperation while falling with the line, now I stalk the world alone and will throughout all time. I cannot control my nature, no wife can bear my seed; to love me is to die by me, our contaversing needs. Who would care to end this? I'm suffering to breathe. All that is left to offer are remains that could lead death back to me.

Eyes transfixed upon stars capture nocturne fire. Gasp to tease my breathing—a beast bound by desire.

With no one to guide me through, I will not trust the gift in you. Remove the pain; make me ash, a return to dust and rest at last.

(Featured on the Scholomance –I Am That Which Is demo 1997)

The Last Agony

Procreation, bear the tears, a trial reaching closure. Accost the youth before they breathe, the filth denies emotion.

Dying elms are whispering, prophetic voices waning. Bow a knee to hypocrisy, the 'messiah' begins the lynching.

Fate now fast approaching, the crow calls out or time. His blackness chills, his shriek rings out, in a tortured child's whine.

Red leaves fall like blood drained saviours to feed what lurks below. Castles loom within the distance, their darkness stains the glow.

Betrayal hides behind the words of all who've crossed my path. They lead themselves to a farce of thrones, preeminence a trap.

An ashen world's inheritance, birthright to this hell—culture dwindles in light of violence, renaissance has failed.

I yearn to reach Last Agony, a state of non-awareness. And with it will be the sorrow felt by others who are jealous.

1998

Anthem of Cries

Claim my discretion, lead me over the falls. Deities profess my beauty in a gazing, belligerent smile. I will not give them vantage. I'll run rebelling in stride. If cornered I'll lash out to sever the ties this mistress of piracy weaves.

Calm winds tame inner seas, vanquish the fever within. Silence the moan I have yet to let out. Leave evident my tolerance of pain. Cranial cremation with every last touch—spell binding, infernal queen. Scornful eyes, losing insight, view the pleasure of slaughter restrained.

Crawl to glorious beatings, callousness in the anthem of cries. Gorgeous are the lacerations—the contrast of colors I've bled. As I reach vulnerability, clarity flees from my thoughts. Engulfed, my senses must have drained, faltering with spilling restraint.

War torn desire and intimacy, mysterious mother of threat; board Xebec from the white beast's mouth—then sink with her lust to new depths.

1998

A Silent Journey

Dance upon nothingness opposing the horizon. Gleaming rays of crystal haunt the vast beyond.

A foreboding constellation sets a sullen mood to his journey. Clouds spill tears and cancer, poisoning the fertile ground.

She becomes a spell that binds him—tied by her shining shackles. Magnetism draws him, abolishing the will to stray.

Winds keep growing stronger, testing his strength to continue. While the Northern flame illuminates the burden he has yet to face.

Condemnation at birth's cry, like some ageless malefaction— inherent asphyxiation by webs within the womb.

Enchantment kindly caresses, upon opening blind eyes to surroundings. Then vision clears to reveal that existence leads him to ruin.

1997

The Inevitable Fall

We measure our progress in terms of destruction, all chained to the moral of systemic corruption. The barb-torn banners of self righteous excuse, the elite are self appointed to thoughtlessly abuse. The hands of our nations are oblivious to the stains, of the bitter red fluid of hypocrisy and pain. We pledge our innocence and declare ourselves immune; with groundless justifications that glorify the ruins. Fall to ruin.

Should we do as we are told when we know that they lie? Are we to benefit from slaughter without ever asking why? Is it true that what is given will come back on us again? Haunting those who inherit systems collapsed from within.

If the lost cower do they achieve anything more, than the brave who rise just to be shattered? We bloat our violent cravings for bloodlust and meat, with the sons and daughters on which the machine incessantly feeds.

Theorize conspiracies, blackened wars promote false security. Are the back-bitten servants indentured or free? Succumb to the control of threats unforeseen. Circumstantial evidence fabricated to bend the collective will. Failures of a hindered education; we are not bred to think, we are bred to kill. The inevitable fall...

Do not let them take your rights. Who are they to take our lives? Propaganda from all sides, to cloud our thoughts, enslaves our minds. See the tower standing tall, encourage indifference in us all. Subservient, will we become? Or crush the project, overcome? Years of progress all in vain... Inject disease to numb the brain. This will all come to an end! This will all come to an end! Oceans rise, they're closing in!! Earth is shifting from within! Hope is burning, hope is lost, this the final holocaust. If we don't consume ourselves, Natures' fury bids farewell.

2001

Section Seven

The Retrograde to my Spirit's Dissolution

Prologue: The New Beginning

There are times in life that can never be planned for, days which are divorced from normality and expectation. These occasions may pass in moments of blurred detail, or as infinities of overwhelming impressions. Rare events like these leave an indelible mark upon the lives of those who experience them, altering or reinforcing their long-held beliefs. Times such as these happen on both sides of consciousness, and transcend fantasy, dreams, or reality—without the bonds and requirements of making orderly sense. Whether taking place within the mind or in the tangible world, or even nearly breaking the line between sanity and some schizophrenic episode, these experiences alter the conclusion of our being. A new beginning to a new ending, opening the doors of the heavens, the gates of our hell, or merely inspiring our creativity and molding our attitudes and perceptions for the remainder of our lives.

I write on this somewhat intangible subject now, having experienced such an occasion recently. Since I have formerly explained the perspective from which the following words were conceived, I would like to provide only this short overview.

This is the transcript of a conversation that I had with a man that I would like to simply refer to as The Other. As you will see, I took a fairly domineering approach in said conversation. Thankfully, I was blessed with a predominantly mild-mannered and attentive listener. One who didn't need so many words to make speaking with him of interest, an entity that asked few questions and only really commented when he had something of worth and insight to say, occasionally disagreeing with skill and eloquence. It is probably of importance to tell the reader that this man seemed very familiar, yet was a stranger to me; more on that déjà vu aspect later. Also, without giving too much away let me include that this conversation began as if it were the continuation to former meetings. If at times it reads as philosophical counterpoint, then realize that is exactly what it was. In that regard, I will provide no immediate setting as philosophy needs none. For now, there is nothing more to add except to state that this is exactly the way the conversation transpired.

<u>Chapter One: The Dream and the Stranger</u>

Christ! I can't believe this! I had that damned dream again. Have I told you about that one?

"I'm not exactly sure that you could have. I don't think we've ever even met. Enlighten me."

It's constantly recurring, with slight deviations that only deepen the mystery of its meaning.

"Sounds interesting, I love a good mystery."

I really don't quite know how much of this I want to share. Great caution must be exercised in the modern environment of 'new age' psychic wannabes and the plethora of would-be Freuds; not to mention the fanatical religious opportunists that would take interpretation for a convenient, quasi-literal spin. For instance, at one point in the subconscious plot, there is revealed a moment of superb advantage for the latter to, as they say, 'run with'.

"I assure you, I am none of the above. My intentions are completely pure. I have always had an interest in the deep feelings and dreams of others; call it a hobby of mine. Tell me about this particular moment in your dream."

I am sitting in what appears to be a classroom. The teacher is asking a few somewhat personal questions, but mostly allowing me to vent my world view pessimism. The strange thing is I can never see the face of the teacher, only the silhouetted figure of a man with his back to me. As I reflect on this aspect of the teachers' anonymity and symbolic shunning, it helps to shed light on the answer to his most direct final question. I do want to point out before revealing the question that this teacher had the air of superiority, even in his silence. It was reminiscent of a visit to a psychiatrist, or maybe a psychologist; not that I've been to either, but I have seen them on TV and that is the referential comparison that he represented. It felt as if my school desk was equipped with a fine and cold leather couch, which could transform and interchange with the surroundings without need for explanation. Anyway, the manner in which the teacher inquired and observed was a definite parallel to my possibly media skewed perception of a visit to the good doctors of mind maintenance. Like I said, the teacher would only occasionally lead me into my outpouring of discontent, my seething accusations of others, my darkest confessions of the crimes of my mind and my flesh. This seemed to go on for awhile, and I became so engrossed in my jaded rant that I ceased to notice the teacher. When I reached the closing comments of this personal trial of the humanity of myself and others, oddly held in a near empty schoolroom, I finally looked to the teacher expecting to find his disinterested back towards me. Upon turning my gaze to the teacher, my body digressed to childhood. Innocence washed over me in waves of brilliance, of brightness, and I felt unnervingly small and insignificant.

In the glorious art of Michelangelo, of Leonardo, of Raphael, he was given life. Standing before me, and above me, and all around me, angelic in power and light, in acceptance and condemnation, in forgiveness with an implied manner of judgment…The Christ of the ideal, the beautifully imagined and European rendered deity. His grace blessed and burned my eyes and my spirit. I was overwhelmed by confusion and revelation, adoration and long conditioned fear. All of this awe-imposed silence was finally broken as his voice came with the soul-splaying weight of authority and the gentle care of a mother's lullaby. One question arose from the well ingrained vision of the manifestation of Christendom—**"Tell me my son, when was it that you lost your Faith?"**

Chapter Two: Issues of Paranoia

"Ok, I can see how your dream could be taken in a literal sense by religious opportunists of the Christian ilk. But, do you honestly feel that many of these folks are even concerned with analyzing your dreams, especially those who don't even know you? It seems to me that there are more important issues for them to contend with."

Actually, I do think that. Call me paranoid, but only after a lifetime of complete strangers feeling the apparent duty to bear witness to me have I reached this conclusion. And I agree that there are bigger social 'fish to fry', although I doubt that our ideas on what those issues are would share any common ground.

"Why do you think people of the faith are so compelled to approach you? What gives them the indication that you aren't already saved?"

Who knows? It's like they have a sixth sense for non-believers. Or perhaps it's a judgmental assumption based on the way I look, the music I listen to, the way I carry myself...I really don't understand it. Maybe I just put off a vibe.

"You do have a bit of a discontented scowl. And you seem as if you might be trying to stand out for that kind of attention. No offense."

...None taken.

"As I was saying, it doesn't take long to figure out your views on life; you seem rather anxious to share them. We just met and look at the personal depths this conversation is already going to. You appear to be very well mannered though. It doesn't come off as an immature maneuver for negative attention. I assume that you truly believe in your way of thinking and want others to know it so they don't offend you. Perhaps this is a way to avoid confrontation."

Or to invite it, that is the occasional result after all. Look, I have no real desire to offend anybody in their religious beliefs; I just want the same respect. I was raised in a very moral Christian environment, and was always taught to treat others with respect.

"Then you came away with the best part of the Christian teachings. Loving others is achieved through showing them respect."

I suppose. It's hard for me to love strangers though, hate seems easier sometimes. Then again that makes me the judgmental and prejudice fool as well, doesn't it? Like Nietzsche warned: 'Beware when fighting monsters not to become one'.

"And, 'when you stare into the abyss it stares back into you'. Well, something to that effect. I have a bit of a personal interest in Nietzsche."

Good, he was brilliant. I never believed that bit about him going insane after Twilight of the Idols and The Antichrist; that just seems too obvious, too beneficial for the powers that be. I smell conspiracy.

"Those books are evidence of his faltering sanity in my opinion. Anyway, we've really strayed from the subject at hand which was the dream and its repercussions."

That's an interesting way to put it...repercussions; in a way that relates quite well to the Nietzsche digression. Can we talk about something else for a while though? This is feeling a bit too personal.

"You like to stay in control don't you?"

I guess in a very unintentional way I could have a slight need for control; it's easier that way.

"That's fine."

Would you like to talk some more or do you have somewhere that you need to be?

"I'm in no hurry to get anywhere."

Chapter Three: The Formalities

So, what's your story? Is there anything that I should know about my most gracious listener?

"Like what?"

You know, where are you from? What do you do for a living? The typical stuff…

"Ah, the formalities…I had hoped that we could continue to avoid the accepted rules of cordial introduction. For instance, we haven't even exchanged names."

My name is James.

"Pleasure, I have a brother named James. As I was saying, this is a refreshing approach to meeting someone; getting right into the interesting and deep aspects of personality and experience, without need for the superfluous."

To each his own I guess. I suppose if we were to take literally some of Jung's theories, not to mention many traditional religious views, we are all related at some level. That somewhat eliminates the possibility of an absolute stranger.

"Exactly! In a way, we already know one another. We've come too far at this point to begin again with gentlemen's tradition in tact. That would seem to be counter-productive."

Honestly, this is the first moment since sitting down next to you and commencing our spontaneous verbal intimacy that I have even noticed our slightly ironic surroundings, or even any visual perception of you. There's just an immediate degree of comfortable recognition and intellectual relation between us. Something akin to running into an old friend who looks completely different than you remember him, yet you know him instantaneously—sort of a spiritual familiarity beyond our usual shallow outer based judgment of 'strangers'.

"I often have that effect on people."

…Seriously? Good. I'm not alone then.

"No, James, you are certainly not alone."

Chapter Four: Divergence

Sometimes I feel that life just can't be real. Perhaps the Hindu myth that we are all just a part of some god's dream contains some truth.

"Some god? Are you trying to tell me that you believe in more than one god?"

Well, I don't know if I would call myself a polytheist or anything like that, but it seems more plausible than to think that there is just one God who is actually three. What a silly way to reconcile the multiple references of other gods contained within the bible. The Trinity also conveniently omits the sacred feminine.

"You can't always look at the highest mysteries with skeptical human eyes. The human mind cannot comprehend such things at this point in its evolution. The Trinity goes beyond simple analysis."

So, you believe in evolution?

"I'll tell you now: I love God, and there is only one true God. He created man with the ability to evolve physically, as well as mentally. Man always seems more predisposed to the former."

Or, as Bill Hicks would say: 'It's time to evolve ideas.'

"Funny man Bill Hicks? A very perceptive young man; unfortunately, he took his own ideas to an early and bitter grave."

That's a bit of a callous statement. Am I to take it that you weren't a fan?

"No, no. That might have come off wrong. Bill was a great man; I just feel as if he encouraged negativity at times, and died young and unhappy. That hardly seems to be a good role model for mental evolution."

Perhaps you are looking at the human condition with skeptical and un-evolved eyes. If a man faces the truth of his social surroundings, that might tend to inspire such bitterness. Would someone like Bill be better off to lie to himself like some foolish priest or two cent preacher?

"You're missing the point! And why do you insist on attacking religion for all of society's woes?"

Because it is at fault! We were abandoned here; orphaned if we are to believe that book of threats and lies. Created as sinners, and for what? Is God a damned sadist? What creature would create us to suffer, to hurt? Religion is at fault! I blame religion and God for my woe, and with justification. I have no need for this tyranny, this holy totalitarianism.

"You were created out of God's all encompassing mercy and love! How can you utter such blasphemy?"

Because I don't believe it! Tell the victims of the flood about God's mercy; the wrath of nature if truth be known.

"If you aren't a believer, then why the anger and passion? People who truly don't believe would have no time to waste on arguing the finer points of Christianity...and why not other religions? You're awfully selective for someone who claims no affiliations."

It is a myth that dominates the good sense of my country and family. Christianity hits home, which is why I gravitate my discontent towards it. If it's any consolation, I disagree with any belief that creates of us servants.

"That is arrogance."

No, that is experience. I have never been in the presence of a higher being. For all of our shortcomings, humans are still the highest species on the planet.

"I quote: 'on the planet'. Don't limit your mind to the minimal wealth of its experience. Am I to assume that you believe in life from other planets?"

Why the hell wouldn't I? It makes too much sense to disagree with. If not, as Sagan said, the universe is a ridiculous waste of space.

"Listen I don't want to argue, only to attempt to understand. I just hope that someday you let go of your anger."

When the unfair judgment and condemnation by others fades, so will my anger.

"You don't have to be a martyr, James."

Nor am I attempting to be.

"And what of your judgment and condemnation of others?"

What of it? Mine is justified.

"Those who you come down upon also feel justified when they stand in judgment."

They're not.

"That remains in the eye of the beholder. It's all a matter of perspective."

'Judge not lest ye be judged.'

"Words to live by…"

Chapter Five: Exposed Nerves

Alright, this little talk of ours seems to have taken a bit of a wrong turn. I guess we each share some exposed nerves when it comes to the religion topic.

"I agree though, to an extent, that some followers can get carried away with 'religion' and miss out on the beauty of spirituality."

Precisely! That's what gets me. There are positive aspects to every religion, and many common ones. The main link would be our spiritual needs. Even though I have no strong faith, I can absolutely vouch for the validity of experience for people who do.

"That's why it's so puzzling that you can't accept it. Obviously it bothers you to not have faith, so much that you can't seem to help verbally attacking those who do have it."

I need facts. Prove it to me. Define 'IT'. That's the only way for my mind and heart to accept it, at least for myself.

"Faith is not based on fact, but incredible belief. The need is not there when you truly believe."

The need is not there when you cease to care either.

"Some day I believe you will know the truth, and at that time you will no longer need stated facts and science. And, quite honestly, from what I can tell, you care too much if anything."

I just cannot understand the optimism that these people can show at the worst of times. Sure, it is to their benefit not to dwell on things, but it also reeks of denial.

"They know that it's all a part of a greater scheme."

…The divine plan?

"…For lack of a better phrase? Absolutely."

How does this plan co-exist with tragedy? It seems cruel to me.

"We are not owed explanations for the way things happen. We have been blessed with life, and with life comes joy and sorrow, triumph as well as tragedy. God endowed us with a planet of choice and free will. All decisions have a possibility of consequence."

There is no reconciliation of this manufactured plan of predestination and free will. One concept is a lie.

"It is not a lie, just beyond ordinary comprehension. God is beyond 'concepts' and 'theories'."

Omniscient, omnipotent, omnipresent: mere words, with no basis in possibility or reality.

"With faith comes understanding."

The answer to everything remains faith to those who deny science. We spoke momentarily of the possibility of life on other planets. That could be the source of all mythology.

"Ah, so you're one of those types?"

I could say the same about you being a Christian.

"Haven't you?"

Chapter Six: On the Topic of Faith

I'm not saying that earthly science can answer all of the major cosmic mysteries, just that it is the best start. We are but a microcosm of our country, our country of our planet, our planet of our solar system, and our solar system of the universe. Just think about it, we are less than sand, if even microscopic, in the universal scheme of things.

"Sounds like more of an argument for belief than science."

Ok, I'll give you that one. I guess it's a good argument for either side. I definitely don't think that any outer space civilizations, no matter how advanced, could answer all of the universal riddles. But, maybe they could answer some of the most relevant ones to our survival. It is possible that the universe is the microcosm to something greater, and maybe that something could be likened to 'god', or a life-force. I don't know, but I don't pretend to, and that is the difference between me and Christians.

"So you admit the possibility of the existence of a form of God?"

Symbolically, yes, not the humanized version of him though. I don't feel that there is some old man in the clouds; nor do I feel that there is some Atlas-modeled macrocosmic being supporting the world, or the universe, with his immense strength. These are merely archaic solutions to the great mysteries. It's too bad that those are the only kind of answers that survived The Church; I feel that the ancients knew more than we are aware of today.

"It always returns to the church doesn't it?"

Well, they did usher in the Dark Ages after all. They repressed the truth at every moment that it contradicted their reign.

"You speak like a true conspiracy theorist; 'they' appear at each bad turn."

Regardless, this is fact—if anything can elevate us to God, or beyond, it is uninhibited science. There should be no further restraints on the truth.

"We agree about the need for truth, but have differing paths to arrive at it. Agree to disagree?"

Of course, this type of philosophizing is quite invigorating. It's rare to have this stimulating of a conversation with everyday friends. Perhaps, I'll seek out strangers more often.

"I'm not your typical stranger, James."

Billions of planets in an infinite universe and we share this small earth as dust through the fingers of gods, nothing more than miniscule, yet capable of greatness. We are all more than strangers, of that I'm sure.

"Waxing poetic are we? We are nearing the end of our time here…Anything more to add prior to revelation?"

Chapter Seven: The Revelatory Façade

Have you ever awoken to find that reality is stranger than any dream? For instance, here's something that I occasionally ponder. If there was an opportunity to travel to the past, the future, or another world or dimension, and speak with beings unfamiliar with our own time about events and technologies current to us, how would they react? If you told a utopian society about the division in our age due to differing belief systems and social classifications, or about the wars we engage in over ideologies, land, fuel and politics, they would never believe you.

If you could travel back through time to tell the Mayan civilization that the rainforest which nurtured their existence, their every need, was being burned to the ground for ranch land—in part by their nearest living descendants—they would never even be able to comprehend such ignorance. As a matter of fact, you'd probably lose your head!

Our understanding is always limited to the possibilities in which we are able to accept.

"Or perhaps to the extent in which we are able to open our minds and hearts…"

Yeah, I'll buy that. Another example is that many people 'believe' in God, but if they claimed in our current society to have seen great miracles, angels, devils, or God himself, many people of the same faith would ridicule them or worse. Very few would be able to accept the second coming of Christ if he ever was to return to earth with his seven trusty seals of retribution. His fate would probably remain the same as before, or at least some modern equivalent of mockery and crucifixion.

"Do you really believe that? I would hope people were beyond all of that inquisitional behavior."

Well, they might not get away with the torturous evil that they perpetuated in the name of righteousness during the inquisition. And, as far as I know, Pilate hasn't been seen of late and the new Roman Empire is the ever God-fearing America. Still yet, with all of the veiled holy wars and modern crusading in the Middle East, it seems plausible to expect irrational and cruel behavior from any fundamentalist believers.

"It's a very sad state in the Middle East, a very sad state indeed. Birthplace of civilization and religions meant to enrich the human experience, instead begetting constant conflict."

"I do have one point of contention, and that is with you spouting that little sarcasm about Pilate. The implication is that he was solely responsible for the crucifixion. He did after all wash his hands of any guilt for what that was worth. The priests—the Pharisees—accepted the bloodied hands for themselves and their children to be ever accursed."

Well, their kind seems to be doing alright at present and, unlike Pilate, they have been and will be present always—these finger-pointing accusers of blasphemy and heresy.

The thing is, in my opinion, the concept of God is just a way to humanize the inexplicable; it is a way to explain that which cannot be explained. Science will always be at war with that kind of dumbing down of the universal mysteries.

"Perhaps it will be, but where does the inspiration for their quest for answers come from? Is there not divinity behind all inspiration?"

I am always inspired and I have no need for a divine explanation or source for it!

"I'm not out to offend you. It's just that I find hope for a better life after this one to be very appealing. How is it that you do not?"

I find honesty is the best policy for making the present and sure life appealing and rewarding.

"Then you are a slave to your own humanity. Your chains are science and logic. Your cell is the very earth. There are no answers without God, no mysteries so great and worthy of acknowledgement and reverence."

Believe me, I want answers. I want truthful explanations for the feats of ancient civilizations. I want to understand the achievements of Egypt, the advanced lifestyle and mythology of Mesopotamia. I have no need for the incessant knowledge suffocation inherent in Christianity or the Islamic faith. I revile this Dark Ages glorification; the endless need for a new holy crusade as opposed to a new and better enlightenment. The oppression of factual scientific and historic knowledge is nothing but a means of control. Humanity should stay far away from such a calculated enslavement at the hands of religious and political figures.

"That might be a bit of an exaggeration of the breadth of the problem. You continue to deal out a pretty serious list of negative implications against religion."

I am just fed up with the arrogance of it all. To think that our fall is possible remains beyond common comprehension, however, I assure you it is not beyond probability.

Do you want to completely lose yourself in the dream of life? Do you need something seriously deep to interpret? Try the concept of infinity. Think about the fact that the universe is expanding and wonder about what used to reside in the area it is, or will be, inhabiting. Dark matter and dark energy make up more of the universe by far than the visible atom-based particles. There is more out there that we can't see than what we can. Innumerable galaxies, yet we are told we are alone? What lies in the blackness beyond the sight of our furthest reaching satellites and telescopes? What is beyond the universe? More universes, other dimensions? What is beyond the beyond and after? Nothingness is not an answer. Even nothing is something.

Just because we don't know the answers, or perhaps even the proper questions, doesn't eliminate the possibilities. We might have been created in God's image, or vise-versa, but that does not make us omnipotent. A concept alone comes into being or ceases to be due to our knowledge, or lack of knowledge, of its existence. The same is not true for the universe and natural things, or perhaps for the supernatural.

All that we know is the finite, all that we can understand is an end and a beginning, that there might not be one is baffling to us; because the life we are currently experiencing will definitely end. As for the possibility of our eternal spirit, that may be the strangest dream of all.

"That is a dream in which I place much faith—the eternal spirit. And, I believe in a truly spiritual state, questions do not need to be answered. In the spiritual realm infinity fades away like all human ideas."

…Seems awfully convenient to me. Anyway, I apologize for the philosophical digression. It's not often that I can vent my thoughts and feelings so freely to someone I've just met. It's just that, as I said before, I sense a strange familiarity with you. Hopefully you don't take me as being too rude. It seems I've somewhat dominated the latter part of the conversation. Nevertheless, I am dying to know a little more concerning you and your feelings about the conversation. I promise not to interrupt with any religion bashing. How about that name now?

"Back to the formalities are we? A conversation in reverse... Honestly, I think that you know my name. After all I do seem very familiar and comfortable to you, as you have implied more than once. I really didn't mind listening to your slightly meandering tirades, for time has little meaning to me. I especially liked the dream sequence early on in our conversation, and the references to infinity, as well as the micro and macrocosms theory. It is very entertaining to hear attempted complexity from such a simple creation. Though, some may find it a pretentious example of mankind's need for explanation."

"I also appreciate the take on hypocrisy within the religious population in regards to the second coming and literal condemnation of others—a total missed message. That is quite possibly the reason for the heavenly apprehension, which you seem to thoroughly enjoy pointing out."

"You should probably check a few facts though before having another long-winded, often one-sided conversation with a more judgmental being than I. I recognized a few misconceptions, and a bit of confusion."

That's a little harsh; after all, I'm only human.

"True, very true indeed. I guess there is just one last question that I need to ask of you and try to keep the answer short and to the point this time."

<u>"Tell me my son, when was it that you lost your faith?"</u>

The Aftermath

The Other allowed no time for my answer. It was as if he simply faded from all view of reality. Only his question burned in my mind propagating more questions, more doubt.

Was it rhetorical, an altered recurrence of the previous dream? I sat there—a splintered individual—feeling insecure in all prior notions of conscious and subconscious perception and separation, literally falling to pieces; what was one could very well have been many.

I felt like screaming, "Come back you bastard! Tell me what it all means! Tell me that I remain who I was, that I remain unchanged. Damnit, I need to know if my sanity is dissolving. What is the line between Truth and Mirage?"

I was left with these parasitic questions devouring my every confidence. Did I gain a new faith or lose a part of myself? Who was I before and what will I be from here on?

The Other, of course, did not come back, and like him I began to fade. All light diminished except for the light of the room we had been in all along. Was that even real? The surroundings that had virtually disintegrated at the advent of our conversation became clear—the retrograde to my spirit's dissolution.

It seemed no surprise to see a classroom coming sharply into focus: the bland tan and cold steel of the school desk, the fluorescent lights that would hum a monotonous tune as our impressionable childhood minds became standardized and subjugated, the screeching blackboard where the half-truths were unceasingly conveyed; no surprise to have been there at all—no shock as my adult life began to digress to the insecurity of adolescence.

This is how I was left; abandoned with that final condescending question, with the stinging last words of a man I had grown to trust in only moments, abandoned in this factory of repressed learning that tormented my youth. I might as well have been in a church...

And I knew that the tone of his voice at the end of our conversation, the change of his manner from gracious and nurturing to judgmental and hardened, echoed his frustration with my skeptical sentiments—mirrored my own social rage.

Just before I surrendered to the momentary oblivion of all awareness, a whisper of recollection hissed The Other's intuitive prophetic phrase: "A conversation in reverse".

Only darkness followed.

Epilogue: Thirteen Days

Thirteen days have passed. The lines between conscious and subconscious reality are still a blur. In retrospect, they were blurred all along. They were a wash of colors even during the documented conversation, thus the lack of setting and tangible description. None was needed. This was utter engrossment in topic. Best set as a transcript, with frames.

I had no answer for the last question of The Other. If I did, there would be no chance of my sharing it now.

I can't help but feel betrayed by the vagueness of that morning, as if I were the pawn in the ongoing chess match of the gods. Answers are never given, only more and more questions; nothing but a new reason for doubt and faith to pick at the spirit—the seeming carrion deity.

At the same time, I wouldn't trade this experience. Even if it was all a dream, when I awake from the disillusion I know that clarity will elevate me to a further evolution.

Despite my resentment at coming so close to the Truth, only to emerge further from it while being forced to recognize the limits of my perceived knowledge, I feel I have gained insight on some level. This experience will have empowered my mind and soul. Some day I will know...

The Last Laugh: A Stinging Review from the Toughest Critic

Upon delving into The Conscience Market by James Christopher Pitts, I was immediately struck with the overwhelmingly obvious contradiction of the whole work. As a rule, I never open a review with immediate criticism; however, in this case it just seems unavoidable. James strikes me immediately as an amateur trying to make a name for himself by blindly attacking our most treasured institutions.

Honestly though, about the time that I think there is not anything held sacred by Mr. Pitts, he'll digress into some mournful and sentimental work of dedication to nature, family, or to one of his many influences; quoting the latter almost verbatim at times without regard for the good manner of credit due

James seems painfully entrenched in a wrestling match between altruism and misanthropy. I am left to speculate about his education in the literary arts, occasionally imagining his flustered English teachers explaining to him that good writing does not consist of ranting tirades and that poetic sentences do not require excessive expletives or complicated terms that everyday people will scarce relate to—or for that matter even care to. I will not even begin to critique the grammar and structure of his work. I do after all have deadlines to meet.

Especially confusing was his short story, and I hesitate to call it that, "The Retrograde to My Dissolution". I am forced to the conclusion that Mr. Pitts has either been diagnosed clinically schizophrenic, or is simply disturbingly confused about the separation between reality and fantasy. What was this effort intended to represent: a short story, a mini-novel, philosophy? Is there room on the already flooded market for something that cannot even be classified by the widely accepted standards of public interest and good taste? Even the title seems exceedingly pretentious. As for "The Other", James imaginary counterpoint in this nonsensical conversation, am I to assume that he is representative of Jesus Christ? Is this an attempt at an artistic statement expressing the abandonment of mankind by God? The whole effort lacks setting, character development, and even the proper assignment of quotations. The conversation is set in the past; like a transcript of a prior conversation, but James leaves the reader to distinguish his character from "The Other," with only the aid of the latter's statements being enclosed in quotation marks. I can't decide if this type of unconventional writing should get at least some credit for originality, or if I should continue on with the trashing.

What is most frustrating about all sections of the book would be the abundant use of questions. Where are the answers? What does Mr. Pitts offer us aside from more doubt and insecurity in the lives we live? For instance, I never ask questions in a book review, yet with <u>The Conscience Market</u> I am forced to ask several. I suppose to summarize my take on James Christopher Pitts' first attempt at being an author I should rightfully end with a question as well. I interrogate this 'poet of questions' by simply asking him: What were you thinking when you penned this nonsense? And, please don't answer with a question.

Reviewed by **James C. Pitts**, November 28, 2004

Printed in the United States
27773LVS00005B/220-318

9 781420 832716